A Most Unsettled State

First-Person Accounts of St. Louis During the Civil War

NiNi Harris

REEDY PRESS
St. Louis, Missouri

Reedy Press
PO Box 5131
St. Louis, MO 63139
www.reedypress.com

Library of Congress Control Number: 2013947198

ISBN: 978-1-935806-55-4

Cover design by Jill Halpin

Printed in the United States of America
13 14 15 16 17   5 4 3 2 1

Note: The letters, articles, journals, and other documents excerpted for this work contain inaccurate or antiquated punctuation, spelling, and vocabulary. That spelling and punctuation has been reproduced as it appeared in the original documents.

The best efforts have been made to decipher faded print, words on wrinkled or damaged paper, and handwriting styles. In rare instances, words or phrases were illegible.

Contents

3   ST. LOUIS ON THE EVE
OF THE CIVIL WAR

7   Galusha Anderson   {description of St. Louis}
8   Thomas Rodgers   {impressions of St. Louis}
10   Sarah Lindsey   {impressions of St. Louis}
12   Charles Johnson and Edward Bates   {visit of the Prince of Wales}
16   Leonard Matthews   {baseball in Lafayette Park}
17   Galusha Anderson   {slave pens}

21   1861

24   Governor Claiborne F. Jackson   {inaugural speech}
27   Thomas T. Gantt   {"a most unsettled state"}
28   James Broadhead   {winter 1861}
32   Captain James Eads   {speech at Soulard Market}
35   Julius Rombauer   {volunteers for the Union}
39   James McDonough   {chief of police}
40   *St. Louis Christian Advocate*   {atmosphere after Fort Sumter}
42   Captain Albert Tracy   {Jefferson Barracks}
44   William Tecumseh Sherman   {Camp Jackson}
52   Sarah Full Hill   {a narrow escape}
54   Newspapers   {Camp Jackson}
56   State Militia Men   {Camp Jackson}
58   Daniel G. Taylor   {mayor of the city of St. Louis}
60   Willis Pritchard   {water works superintendent}
61   *St. Louis Christian Advocate*   {a violent incident}

62   Leonard Matthews   {buying a substitute}
64   Robert Campbell   {business paralyzed}
66   Jessie Benton Fremont and General John C. Fremont
    {atmosphere and martial law}
71   Sarah Full Hill   {John C. Fremont}

73   1862

76   Sarah Full Hill   {Soldiers' Aid Society}
78   Galusha Anderson   {soldiers, wounded, and contrabands}
82   Ernst Kargau   {business climate}
84   An Unknown Soldier   {Benton Barracks}
87   Daniel G. Taylor   {mayor of the city of St. Louis}
90   John How, John Riggin, and W. Patrick   {police commissioners}
93   Bernard G. Farrar   {loyalty oath}
94   The Louis Picot Family   {confiscation and banishment}
96   Louis Philip Fusz   {funeral of Mrs. P. Chouteau Jr.}
98   The Fashionable Secesh of St. Louis   {gossipy letters}
104   James M. Carpenter   {draft, inflation, and assessments}
107   Absalom C. Grimes   {prison escape}

111   1863

113   Frederick Law Olmsted   {impressions of St. Louis}
118   Emily Elizabeth Parsons   {nursing wounded}
123   Anne Ewing Lane   {resentment and racism}
128   Julia Dent Grant   {the fall fo Vicksburg}
130   Edward Bates   {speech at Carondelet boatyard}
136   *Daily Missouri Democrat*   {reports on Hyde Park riot}
144   Sarah Full Hill   {boatyard boarding house}
147   Joseph A. Fardell   {Invalid Corps}
149   William Greenleaf Eliot   {Sanitary Commission letter}
151   James E. Yeatman, George Partridge, John B. Johnson, Carlos S. Greeley, and William G. Eliot   {Sanitary Commission}

154 1864

157	Ann Valentine	{enslaved in Missouri}
159	Louis Philip Fusz	{enemies in church}
162	Julia Dent Grant	{Confederate neighbor}
164	Galusha Anderson	{Sanitary Fair}
167	Hugh Campbell	{stagnant commerce}
169	Louis Philip Fusz	{Lincoln's re-election}

176 1865

178	John Bates Johnson	{Missouri as a free state}
179	Lillie Balmer Unger	{German-style bribery}
180	Louis Philip Fusz	{views on Lincoln}
182	Galusha Anderson	{Lee's surrender and Lincoln's assassination}
186	The Reverend Samuel J. Niccolls	{Lincoln's assassination}
190	Sarah Full Hill	{the war's end}

ACKNOWLEDGMENTS

The following individuals helped locate and access historical materials:

St. Louis Public Library staff members: Cynthia Millar, Nancy Oliver and Tom Pearson in the Genealogy Room; Adele Heagney and Kirwin Roach in the St. Louis Room; Renee Jones in Special Collections; Louise Powderly in the History Room; Bill Olbrich in the Business, Government & Law Room; Byron Caskey of Support Services, who assisted with great kindness and competence; and the late Keith Zimmer.

Missouri History Museum Library and Archives staff members: Jamie Bourassa, Molly Kodner, Emily Troxell Jaycox, Dennis Northcott, and Carol Verble.

John Waide, archivist at Pius XII Memorial Library, Saint Louis University.

Andrew W. Hahn, director of Campbell House Museum.

Editorial input was provided by Emma Prince and Norm Woldow.

And special thanks to Kathy Kasznel, without whom this book would not have been possible.

A Most Unsettled State

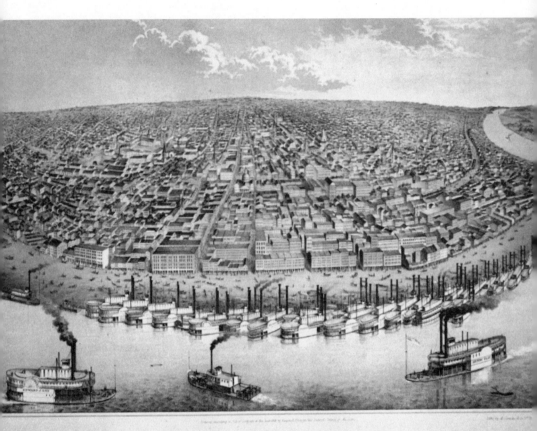

OUR CITY,

(ST. LOUIS. MO.)

St. Louis, 1859. Courtesy Library of Congress

St. Louis on the Eve of the Civil War

Americans knew St. Louis as its riverfront—that piece of real estate that several generations of explorers, soldiers, prospectors, and settlers had funneled through. They knew that paddle-wheelers, moored nose to the levee, lined the riverfront. Sometimes the boats were two deep, so that passengers had to cross the deck of another boat before they could disembark. Stacks of barrels, crates, and bales were piled high on the stone-covered levee. Horses pulled drays through the paths between the stacks. Rows of warehouses lined the narrow and steep streets leading from the levee.

Charles Dickens and Francis Parkman had described that riverfront. Robert E. Lee had directed its reconstruction and paving in the 1840s. Samuel Clemens piloted and helped moor riverboats on it.

Largely unknown, however, was the surrounding metropolis that was powering that famous riverfront. It was a metropolis of over 160,000 residents, the eighth largest city in the United States in 1861.

St. Louis could have been considered a foreign city, since the majority of its population was born outside of the United States.

Nearly 60,000 St. Louisans had emigrated from Germany. They surrounded the town with their beer gardens. Black bread and sausage was their fare. They built Lutheran and Catholic churches, square and uncompromising. At their turnverein, they kept their mother tongue, their music, their culture, and their commitment to democracy alive. They found slavery despicable.

More than 39,000 St. Louisans were natives of Ireland. Thousands of Irish fleeing the potato famine had arrived impoverished and uneducated. At first they built shanties, but soon they were building Catholic churches. They dug ditches and carried hods. This influx of cheap laborers cut the demand for slave labor.

The population included nearly two thousand emigrants from Bohemia who had already formed a brotherhood and established the first Bohemian-Catholic parish outside of Bohemia. On Christmas Eve, the bell echoed from the small frame St. John Nepomuk Church at Eleventh and Lafayette streets, calling the parishioners to church where they sang the Czech cycle of Christmas hymns.

The foreign-born community included a settlement of Swiss immigrants who had begun dairy farms on Gravois near Magnolia, French-born St. Louisans, and a small number of emigrants from Poland.

The American-born population was not homogeneous either. The roots of St. Louisans born and raised in the Eastern states were divided between the Northern and Southern states. The once independent town of Old North St. Louis, around North Market and Broadway, had so many transplants from New England that the town was nicknamed Lowell for Lowell, Massachusetts. The political philosophies of the New Englanders were radically different than those of the Virginians, and natives of the Carolinas who had relocated to the river town.

Among the American born were also second-generation Irish and second-generation Germans who, though born in St. Louis, enjoyed their distinctive cultures and worshipped at their national churches.

Descendants of our early French settlers were prominent among American-born St. Louisans. Their culture and business associations tied St. Louis with the Deep South.

The 1860 Census counted amongst the people living in the city of St. Louis 1,755 "free colored" and 1,542 slaves. The early French and Creoles (people of French or Spanish heritage born in the Americas) had practiced slavery and made slavery an accepted part of the local culture. The French, however, accepted manumission, or freeing of slaves. This resulted in a community of Freedmen, or free African-Americans living alongside African-Americans who were living in slavery.

In 1850, as many as thirty slave dealers operated in St. Louis. The City Directory nine years later listed only Bernard Lynch and one other slave dealer.

St. Louisans found work as roustabouts on the riverboats, or working in the warehouses that supplied westward migration with guns, traps, cutlery, rope, fabric, coffee, spices, pots, dishes, cast iron stoves, brooms, and plows. Many St. Louisans were craftsmen or tradesmen. Their ranks included teamsters, blacksmiths, coopers, stone and brick masons, carpenters, furniture makers, and saddle and harness makers. The growing industries of iron mills, breweries, glass factories, cordage mills and tobacco warehouses employed many new arrivals to the city.

On the eve of the Civil War, the population included Eduard Sobolewski, who was conducting and directing the new St. Louis Philharmonic Orchestra. The European-trained composer and conductor had studied in Dresden and conducted at Weimar at the invitation of Franz Liszt.

Ulysses S. Grant had farmed in South St. Louis County, then worked for a real estate concern and lived in the Soulard neighborhood. After failing at both endeavors, the man who would soon be commanding the entire Union Army left town to take a job clerking in his father's tannery in Galena, Illinois.

William Tecumseh Sherman, who would soon command the Union Army in the West, arrived in St. Louis just before hostilities broke out. He rented his family a home on the 1000 block of Locust Street, while he took the job as president of the Fifth Street Railroad.

The widow of the famous slave Dred Scott, Harriet, made her home in St. Louis and worked as a laundress. The Scotts had been freed, though the court system had failed them in their eleven-year legal battle to win their freedom. The court's decision against the Scotts had widened the national chasm over slavery.

The results of the presidential election in November of 1860 demonstrated how St. Louis had evolved. It also put the city in a precarious position with the rest of the state of Missouri. In 1860 only 1 percent of St. Louis City's population were enslaved. This contrasted sharply with the Little Dixie area of Missouri along the Missouri River, where 29 percent of the population were enslaved African-Americans.

German-Americans had carried the city of St. Louis for Abraham Lincoln, who won with 9,484 votes. Stephen Douglas received 8,538 votes, John Bell received 4,533 votes, and radical Southerner John Breckenridge received only 544 St. Louis votes. By contrast, of the four candidates for president, Lincoln had ranked the lowest in the state. Only 11 percent of Missourians voted for Lincoln. That was remarkably low considering it included the substantial count in St. Louis.

Lincoln's victory inflamed the hostile feelings between North and South and instigated the Secession Winter. On December 20, 1860, the state of South Carolina walked out of the Union. Soon, the six cotton states of Mississippi, Florida, Alabama, Georgia, Louisiana, and Texas seceded. Following the firing on Fort Sumter, Virginia, Arkansas, Tennessee, and North Carolina seceded.

Both the Union and the new Confederacy coveted St. Louis, with its strategic location and its military posts. St. Louis's placement on the Mississippi River made it crucial to maintaining all the border states in the Union. Jefferson Barracks was located just ten miles downriver from the city. Established in 1826, it was the largest military post in the West. The prized federal arsenal was located in South City (at South Broadway across from Anheuser-Busch Brewery). Also established in 1826, it held a treasure trove of arms.

On the eve of hostilities, St. Louis was one of the largest cities of a slave state, tied politically and economically to the North and to the South. It was critical to the Union and critical to the Confederacy.

GALUSHA ANDERSON

alusha Anderson (1832–1918) served as the pastor at the Second Baptist Church of St. Louis, located at the corner of Sixth and Locust streets, from 1858 to 1866. This native of New York wrote a vivid description of the physical makeup of St. Louis on the eve of the Civil War.

Most of the city stood then, as now, on bluffs or extended terraces that rise gradually one above the other. Its situation is both healthful and beautiful. But before the war its area was comparatively small . . . The city was built of brick. The business blocks, warehouses, hotels, residences, schoolhouses, and churches were all of the same material. Most of the sidewalks were also made of red brick. Whichever way you looked your eyes rested on red brick, and wherever you walked you trod on red brick. I remember but one business block that had a stone front, and that was marble. The enterprising citizen who built it made quite a fortune out of it. Its very novelty made it attractive, and its rooms were readily rented to professional men . . .

Most of the dwelling-houses were built out to the street, so that, with rare exceptions, there were no front yards. On warm summer evenings the families living in any given block sat on the front stone steps of their houses, that they might be refreshed by the cooler air of the evening.

Galusha Anderson, The Story of a Border City During the Civil War *(Boston: Little, Brown, and Company, 1908), 2.*

THOMAS RODGERS

Thomas Rodgers of Pittsburgh described the St. Louis he experienced between 1857 and 1860. In his recollections, he seemed surprised at the variety of activities permitted on Sundays. His description of the levee captures the historic energy of that piece of real estate.

I discovered that this was not a Puritan town. I was awakened by the newsboys crying the "Republican" and the "Leader" (it was Sunday). . . . Then I discovered that the saloons were open all day on Sunday, and some theatres; in short that this was rather a "wide open town." I do not remember that there was any great amount of disorder connected with the open saloons. There were also a number of beer gardens in the suburbs, which were open until a late hour, and the "habitues" were regaled with the music of brass bands every Sunday night.

Thomas L. Rodgers, "Recollections of St. Louis, 1857-60," unpublished manuscript, page 1, Missouri History Museum Archives.

The old Levee was an "epitome" of the commerce of this immense [river] system, and in the business season of the year, was, I think, the most inspiring sight on this continent. For more than a mile it was thickly lined with steamers loading and unloading the products of the West and East, and for all that distance one could walk over the piles of produce and not need to set foot on the ground. There were bales of hemp, hogsheads of tobacco, piles of bacon, huge piles of grain in bags, and boxes, bales etc. of merchandise.

Rodgers, "Recollections," 6.

Sarah Lindsey

Sarah Lindsey, a Quaker, kept a journal while she traveled around the country. Her travels included a visit to St. Louis in April 1858. During her visit, she stayed with the family of Robert Campbell at 20 Lucas Place (now the Robert Campbell Museum at 1508 Locust Street). A native of Northern Ireland, Campbell had begun his American career in the Rocky Mountain fur trade.

In her journal entries of April 24 and April 26, Lindsey writes about the Campbells. She explains that Mrs. Campbell's mother had been a Quaker and mentions the Campbells' attitude toward slavery. She describes their elegant home and the city as a whole. This visitor used the term "suburb" to describe residential areas, now part of Downtown St. Louis.

24th, 4 mo — . . . Called upon the widow Lucy Ann Kyle, whose maiden name was Whinstone: she was married to a non-member in early life by which act she lost her membership in our society but her principles seem to accord with our own. She resides with her son-in-law, Robert Campbell, whose wife is her daughter. (Robert Campbell) has lived here many years & is a successful merchant. . . .

26th, 4 mo. — . . . Spent the evening & lodged at R Campbell's, where we met with every comfort & convenience that we could desire. They have a large house & furnished in English style. At one time they held a few slaves but Virginia Campbell not liking the system, nor the care of young negroes, they were set free. Their servants at the present time are Swiss, German & Irish . . .

27th, 4 mo. — Third day. We did not sail until 1/2 past six last evening when we took a final leave of St. Louis, which is a fine & flourishing City. . . . Near the river, and in the business part of the City the streets are ill paved & dirty but the suburbs behind the town contain many good & well built houses chiefly of brick which are painted. The roads are clean, wide, & well paved, & trees planted at intervals. Some of the best houses have gardens attached, in one of which I noticed a bed of tulips in full bloom. Beds of coal & stone are in the neighbourhood.

Robert Campbell papers, Campbell House Museum.

Charles Johnson and Edward Bates on the Visit of the Prince of Wales

O ne of the last great civic festivities to occur in St. Louis before the Civil War was the visit of Albert Edward, Prince of Wales, on September 26–28, 1860. The rosy-cheeked prince, an undergraduate at Cambridge, was touring Canada and the United States.

He arrived on the evening of Wednesday, September 26, on the palatial steamboat City of Alton. He stayed at Barnum's Hotel on Second and Walnut streets, which was managed by a brother of showman Phineas T. Barnum. His trip coincided with the week-long Agricultural and Mechanical Fair. The site of the annual fair, first held in 1856, was the 131-acre square on North Grand Boulevard at Natural Bridge (the site of Fairground Park since 1908). The 150,000 people who packed the fairgrounds hoped for a glimpse of the royal guest.

City Attorney Charles P. Johnson, who later served as lieutenant governor, recalled the commotion surrounding the visit decades later. His memories of the discussion of proper attire and the behavior of the crowds reflected the anxiety over the royal trip, and over the politics of the new citizens.

Thousands of St. Louisans had emigrated from Ireland after the famine. The memory of England's cruel rule over a starving Ireland was fresh in their memories.

Albert Edward, Prince of Wales, on the cover of Harper's Weekly, *October 5, 1860, just one week after his visit to St. Louis. Courtesy Library of Congress*

CHARLES JOHNSON

I recall that Mayor Filley, who was a very plain and democratic man, was anxiously exercised over a fine point of etiquette. It was whether the chief executive of a sovereign American city should so far commit himself to aristocratic usages as to don, in deference to the future ruler of a monarchy, a pair of white kid gloves. . . . It was finally decided that not only should the Mayor equip himself with these effete coverings for the hands, but that all of the delegation should follow his example.

So, on the morning of Sept. 27, when we lined up at the city hall to walk to Barnum's Hotel, all of us wore white kid gloves, and besides had decked ourselves out in our very best clothes. We had considerable trouble in persuading the Judge of the City Court, Thomas J. Daly, member of an influential family of politicians, to accompany us. The great Irish famine had occurred recently and Irish lecturers had circulated through the West, relating the woes of their country and soliciting subscriptions for the starving Irish. Daly, an Irishman, was loath to take part in a function in honor of the son of Queen Victoria, but was finally persuaded to attend. The argument with which he was won over was that he would not be present as an individual but as an official representing a city which could not be lax in offering hospitality to a stranger. This plea of hospitality was one which his Irish chivalry could not resist.

Not only was Johnson concerned with the behavior of angry Irish immigrants, he feared the ruffians from the riverboats and gambling houses might disrupt the festivities.

There was a great crowd along the streets. . . . It was a gala day, for it was Fair Week, and the town was filled with visitors. The river element was very strong here then; the river men were often rather rough characters and terribly outspoken. From them, it was thought, any disturbance would probably rise, if any occurred. . . . [The city] ran wide open, and I remember that there was a row of gambling houses operating full blast along Fourth street.

Our most imposing equipage in those days was a huge carriage, the pride of Jesse Arnot, who ran a famous livery stable on Chestnut street. It was brought forth only on state occasions, and made a regal spectacle, with its plumes and its four splendid black horses. This was the vehicle in which the Prince rode, and the reins were handled by no other than Arnot himself—one potentate paying his respects to another.

I was watching mostly to see whether any ebullition might break forth, and kept an eye on several of our Irish fellow citizens whom I saw in the throng. To my relief, these gentlemen applauded the Prince as much as anyone; in them the spirit of hospitality over bore for the time the feeling of national resentment.

Johnson found the menu for the dinner and the reaction of the future Edward VII to the fare memorable.

Afterwards the Prince was escorted to the lunchroom, where, as a special mark of esteem, he was regaled with delicacies peculiar to the West. The menu included buffalo tongue, quail and prairie chicken, which the Prince tasted with imperturbable urbanity, as he did also the Missouri wines offered to him.

St. Louis Post-Dispatch, *June 29, 1919, C5.*
A Former Prince of Wales and a St. Louis Mayor's White Kid Gloves
Quotes from former Lieutenant Governor Charles P. Johnson recalls visit of
Albert Edward, then Prince of Wales.

EDWARD BATES

The law office of Edward Bates, who would be appointed U.S. Attorney General by Abraham Lincoln, was just south of the Old Courthouse, on South Broadway [then Fifth Street]. Bates was among the civic leaders who greeted the Prince and escorted him to the fair grounds. Bates seemed relieved when he made an entry in his diary extolling the outstanding behavior of the "promiscuous crowd." Promiscuous in 19th century use described a heterogeneous or haphazardly mixed crowd.

. . . everything . . . was conducted decently and in order—more so than was expected, considering the large and promiscuous crowd. . . . The Prince and suite attended the Fair to day. I was one selected to go with them, and, with Col Rob. Campbell, rode out and in the same carriage with Lord St. Germain. They seemed highly pleased with the exhibition, and especially with the order and decorum of the immense crowd . . . drawn by curiosity, to see the Prince and his nobles. Lord St. Germain said to me that he never saw a large, promiscuous crowd so well-dressed and well-behaved.

William R. Nester, From Mountain Man to Millionaire, 2d ed
(Columbia: University of Missouri Press, 2011), 210.

LEONARD MATTHEWS

Leonard Matthews was a broker and banker who, in 1870, co-founded a firm with General A. G. Edwards. On the eve of the Civil War, however, the Baltimore native was the owner operator of a wholesale drug business. He was also a baseball enthusiast and member of the first baseball club in St. Louis, the Cyclone Club, founded in 1859. In his autobiographical notes, Matthews wrote about the Cyclone Club on the eve of the Civil War. He mentions Edward Bredel Jr., a member of a slave-owning family who would join the Confederacy, and John Riggin, who would become a staff officer in the army of General Ulysses S. Grant.

In the early days in St. Louis my most intimate young men friends were John Riggin, Louis Hutchinson, John Stetinius and Paul Prewett, all "high rollers," except myself. We belonged to the St. Louis Cyclone Base Ball Company in 1860. We leased what is now Lafayette Park. At that time, it was surrounded by an osage orange hedge. We spent $600 to put the grounds in shape. This company was one of the first of its kind, formed long before the game became professional. The members were all young men in business, or sedentary life, and the club was for exercise, recreation and social intercourse. . . . One afternoon some of us, Ed. Bredell among the rest, were lying in the shade of the hedge, pitching a ball from one to the other, when someone remarked—"Boys, we will soon have another kind of ball to pitch"—and poor Ed. caught one in battle in Virginia, early in the war.

Leonard Matthews, A Long Life in Review: Autobiographical Notes, *(Privately Printed with the Author's permission in anticipation of his 100th birthday, December 17, 1928), 69; St. Louis Public Library.*

Galusha Anderson

The Second Baptist Church was a plain, steepleless, brick meetinghouse, painted lead color. In that church, Galusha Anderson preached to his congregation, of rich and poor who sat side by side.

Near the church was Lynch's slave pen. Galusha recalled the cruel scene of the enslaved being driven through the streets.

He recalled taking a group of visiting ministers, enamoured by their visit to the South, on a tour of the slave pen. His graphic picture of the pen is in stark contrast to the images of baseball in Lafayette Park.

When in my pulpit, facing my congregation, I also faced, only half a square away, a hideous slave-pen. It was kept by Mr. Lynch, an ominous name. I sometimes saw men and women, handcuffed and chained together, in a long two-by-two column, driven in there under the crack of the driver's whip, as though they were so many colts or calves. Had they committed any crime? Oh, no, they had been bought, in different parts of the State, by speculators, as one would buy up beef-cattle, and were kept in the pen to be sold to the good people of St. Louis and of the surrounding towns and country districts; and those not thus disposed of were bought by slave-dealers for the New Orleans market.

In 1859, some preachers from the eastern States, who had been at New Orleans, attending the annual meeting of the Young Men's Christian Association of the United States, on their return to their homes, stopped for three or four days in our city. They painted in glowing terms the lavish and delicate hospitality that they had received in the commercial capital of Louisiana. Appreciating the truth of all they said, I nevertheless asked them if they visited the famous slave-market of that city. They said that they did not. I affirmed that they had missed a great opportunity of seeing the other side of the picture; that when they had seen and experienced the Christian hospitality of that old Spanish and French city, they ought also to have viewed in contrast a slave auction there—as heartless and cruel a scene as the wide earth afforded. Regretting that they had so superficially done New Orleans, they said, "Have you any slave-markets here?" I replied, "We have some slave-pens, but they are as paradise to perdition to the slave-market down there. Nevertheless, to-morrow I will show you the sights, slave-pens included."

In the morning, three or four of the residents of the city joined us, so that we had a party of nine. We first visited the Mercantile Library with its treasures of art. "Now," I said, "since we are always impressed by contrasts, let us go from tasteful rooms, books and art to Lynch's slave-pen." All were agreed, and we were soon on our way. I had some slight acquaintance with Mr. Lynch, having often spoken to him as he sat out on the sidewalk in warm weather before his pen. He was sitting there when we arrived. "Good morning, Mr. Lynch," I said, "these gentlemen wish to go into your slave-pen." "Certainly," he said, "gentlemen, I am glad to see you." He evidently thought that we had come to trade with him. As we entered the room immediately in front of the pen, one of the party, a tall ungainly-looking lawyer, full of humor and fun, said, "Mr. Lynch, look out for these fellows, they are a pack of abolitionists." Lynch received the declaration simply as a chaffing joke and laughed heartily. It was, however, sober truth. He put his great iron key into the lock, turned back the bolt, swung open the door, and turning his face towards us, said, "Gentlemen, I have not much stock on hand to-day." Every man in our company was shocked beyond expression by that brutal announcement. We filed solemnly in. He shut the door and left us alone and undisturbed to examine his "stock." The room was in shape a parallelogram. It was plastered and had one small window high up near the ceiling.

There was no floor but the bare earth. Three backless, wooden benches stood next to the walls. There were seven slaves there, both men and women, herded together, without any arrangement for privacy. Some of the slaves were trying to while away their time by playing at marbles. One fairly good-looking woman about forty years old, tearfully entreated us to buy her, promising over and over again to be faithful and good. In that sad entreaty one could detect the harrowing fear of being sold down South. Her plaint was more than a good pastor from Troy, N.Y., could endure. Coming up close to my side he said, "For God's sake, Anderson, let us get out of here!" I rapped on the door; Mr. Lynch opened it; we thanked him for his kindness, bade him good day, and marched silently down the street. There was now no joking, no merriment. We turned the corner into another street. We were hidden from Lynch's gaze. My friend from Troy stopped; in indignation he stamped his foot; he was in agony of spirit; he planted his heel on the brick sidewalk and, turning the toe of his foot hither and thither again and again, he ground the brick under his heel. It was an instinctive bodily movement, an irrepressible outward expression of his intense desire to grind slavery to powder. At last he exclaimed, "Thank God, I never had anything to do with that." "Don't be too sure about that," I replied, "how have you voted?" . . .

Later, Anderson described another slave pen at Fifth and Myrtle streets "where they keep little colored boys and girls for sale."

This pen where slave children were kept was much larger than Lynch's. The traffic in children seemed to be specially brisk and profitable. The inmates of this grim prison-house were from about five to sixteen years old. Both sexes were there. When the slave-trader bought a mother and her children, she was sometimes for a season shut up with her brood in that hated place. Every few weeks there was an auction of these black children, with all of its repulsive, heart-breaking scenes. On one such occasion the auctioneer commended to a crowd a beautiful mulatto girl, about sixteen years old, as having the blood of a United States senator running in her veins. Some in that gaping throng listened with delight; but a gentleman from the East, a mild-mannered man, unexpectedly flamed out with indignation, and denounced the auctioneer and the whole vile slave-trade. For this drastic, burning denunciation he was threatened with violence. But this man of gentle spirit and manners, when aroused, proved to be a veritable "son of thunder," and he defied his assailants. "When," he said, "this shameless injustice is not only periodically enacted in our city, but our whole State is plunged into ignominy by offering for sale a daughter of a United States senator, I cannot and will not hold my peace. Do what you please. I denounce the outrage." Those that threatened him were cowed into silence; the disturbance was only a momentary ripple; the auctioneer went on with his nefarious task; the girl with senatorial blood was knocked down to the highest bidder. And then another, and another, and another, boy or girl, was sold under the hammer till the fall of the curtain of darkness put temporary end to the shameless work.

Anderson, 152-186.

1861

"All the past we leave behind with Sumter."
—*Walt Whitman*

When the year dawned, scores of young men living at the Lutheran seminary on Jefferson Avenue in South St. Louis were studying Latin and Greek classics, theology, and philosophy. By September, the green lawns of Lafayette Park had been transformed into a dusty camp for hundreds of young men who had volunteered to bear arms for the Union.

As St. Louisans tried to celebrate the new year of 1861, anxiety, apprehension, and fear permeated their mood.

St. Louisans were divided and their new governor was a secessionist. The devotion of St. Louis's large German community to the Union and abolition seemed to feed the hatred of the growing anti-foreign movement. The nation was tearing itself apart, and St. Louis's location on the banks of the Mississippi made it key to both the Union and the rebelling Southern states.

This geography and the citizens' divided loyalties made St. Louisans realize the gravity of the situation. While many Americans on both sides of the issues believed that glorious and decisive battles would end a conflict in a season, St. Louisans talked of potential war with terrible dread. Local attorney Thomas T. Gantt wrote of "unspeakable evils which will flow from such a struggle..."

While Southern states were seceding, an exhausting whirlwind of political and military events blew through St. Louis. Political adversaries held hostile meetings, rallies, elections, and conventions both statewide and in wards throughout the city. At stake at these ward-level meetings was the fate of St. Louis, the state of Missouri, and ultimately, the United States.

The Minute Men—five hundred men who supported secession—drilled at the Berthold Mansion at Fifth and Pine streets. The Wide-Awakes and the Committee of Safety, both supporting the Union, met and drilled at the Turnverein, a German gymnastic and cultural association at Tenth and Market streets. Their numbers grew to over fourteen hundred men, mostly Germans. Eventually they drilled not only at the Turnverein, but also in foundries, in breweries, in Yaeger's Garden in Soulard, and even at Washington Hall on the riverfront.

Influential national political leaders were still attempting to reunite the nation when secessionists fired on the federal Fort Sumter. The attack on Fort Sumter on April 12, 1861, propelled the nation irrevocably into war.

In St. Louis, increasingly armed camps focused on control of the federal Arsenal, the largest arsenal west of the Mississippi. Located between South Broadway and the Mississippi River at Arsenal Street, its supply of weapons could equip a small army. Behind the scenes, Congressman-elect Frank Blair and other Union supporters had quietly negotiated the transfer of the command of the Arsenal from Southern-sympathizing officers to ardent Unionist Nathaniel Lyon.

In May, hostilities over the supply of weapons erupted. Ironically, the violence occurred neither at the pro-Confederate State Militia Camp (Camp Jackson) near Grand and Lindell boulevards nor at the Arsenal. Instead, Union volunteers, mostly Germans, had surrounded Camp Jackson and accepted the militia's surrender. While marching their secessionist militia prisoners back to the Arsenal, angry citizens supporting secession harrassed the Union volunteers. Inexperienced volunteers, threatening crowds, and confusion devolved. Troops fired at the mob on the streets of St. Louis, and the confrontation became known as the "Battle of Camp Jackson." While outbreaks of violence continued after Camp Jackson, St. Louis was aligning itself with the Union.

St. Louis business was being shut down by the closing of the Mississippi as war news poured in from across the state.

Federal troops were pitted against pro-secessionist State Guard or militia led by Governor Claiborne Fox Jackson and General Sterling Price. Union General Nathaniel Lyon drove the State Legislature from the capitol at Jefferson City on June 15. This military victory cleared the path for political change that kept Missouri from seceding. The Missouri State Convention, which had been called to consider secession, reassembled and found Governor Claiborne Jackson guilty of treason. The convention established a provisional Unionist state government and elected conservative Unionist Hamilton Gamble governor.

July 1861 also brought upheavals and changes at national and local levels. The news from the East sent shudders through Union supporters and bouyed local Confederate sympathizers. Thirty-seven thousand Union troops had confidently marched into the state of Virginia. On July 21, Confederate forces lining Bull Run Creek routed the Federal Army.

The glamorous Major General John C. Fremont, known as "The Pathfinder" for his adventures in the West, took command of the Western Department, headquartered in St. Louis. He changed not just the atmosphere, but the physical character of St. Louis, building barracks, forts, and hospitals.

Security measures changed day-to-day life. All civilians leaving St. Louis or the county were required to show passes, in accordance with a directive stating that there was evidence that individuals were "daily leaving this city for the purpose of treasonably communicating with the enemy, and giving them information, aid, and comfort, in violation of the law." Over 85,000 passes were issued during the next three months. Checkpoints were established and baggage inspected at all ferries, train stations, steamboat landings, and major roads leading to county.

On August 10, the Federals were defeated and Lyon killed at Wilson Creek near Springfield. As wounded Union soldiers from Wilson Creek were transported to St. Louis, the price of the Civil War became frighteningly clear. At the end of the month, Fremont declared marshal law.

Fremont was constantly at odds with superior officers and public figures. In November, General Henry W. Halleck replaced the flamboyant Fremont. Although Fremont commanded great loyalty of his German-American soldiers, he had left Missouri further polarized and the Western Department in disarray.

At the end of 1861, the city of St. Louis was faced with its southern trade cut off, cumbersome security measures to keep the locals from supporting the South, and refugees filling its streets. The year ended with the grim reality of war.

The year 1861 left St. Louis forever changed.

Governor
Claiborne F. Jackson

On January 3, 1861, Kentucky native Claiborne Fox Jackson was inaugurated governor of Missouri. In his inaugural address, he warned the federal government against coercion. Parts of the speech sounded like a rallying cry for secession. The following passages from the speech define the issue for the state of Missouri as slavery.

The destiny of the slave-holding States of this Union is one and the same. So long as a State continues to maintain slavery within her limits, it is impossible to separate her fate from that of her sister States who have the same social organization. . . . In the event of a failure to reconcile the conflicting interests which now threaten the disruption of the existing Union, interest and sympathy alike combine to unite the fortunes of all the slaveholding States. The identity, rather than the similarity, of their domestic institutions—their political principles and party usages—their common origin, pursuits, tastes, manners, and customs—their territorial contiguity and intercommercial relations—all contribute to bind them together in one brotherhood the States of the South and South-West. . . .

THE BATTLE OF BOONEVILLE, OR THE GREAT MISSOURI 'LYON' HUNT.

The Battle of Booneville (sic), or the Great Missouri "Lyon" Hunt, Currier & Ives, 1861, depicts General Nathaniel Lyon routing Governor Jackson (in skirt and bonnet) and General Sterling Price (right). Courtesy Library of Congress.

Missouri, then, in my opinion will best consult her own interests and the interest of the whole country, by a timely declaration of her determination to stand by her sister slave-holding States, in whose wrongs she participates, and with whose institutions and people she sympathizes. . . .

So far as Missouri is concerned, I do not fear to misrepresent the sentiments of her citizens by saying that they have ever been devoted to the Union, and will remain in it, so long as there is any hope of its maintaining the spirit and guaranties of the Constitution. But if the Northern States have determined on putting the slave-holding States on a footing of inequality, by interdicting them from all share in the Territories acquired by the common blood and treasure of all—if they have resolved to admit no more slave-holding States into the Union . . . if they mean to persist in nullifying that provision of the Constitution which secures to the slave-holder his property, when found within the limits of States which do not recognize it, or have abolished it—they have themselves practically abandoned the Union, and will not expect our submission to a government on terms of inequality and subordination.

Compiled and Edited by Buel Leopard, A.M., and Floyd C Shoemaker, A.M., Secretary of the State Historical Society of Missouri, The Messages and Proclamations of the Governors of the State of Missouri, *Vol. III (Columbia, Missouri, 1922), 333, 335.*

THOMAS T. GANTT

On January 5, 1861, attorney Thomas T. Gantt wrote to his neighbor, leading businessman Robert Campbell, concerning his fears of Southern secession. Gantt had served as U.S. District Attorney for the District of Missouri and city counselor for the city of St. Louis. He was an Unconditional Union man. In a mere paragraph in the letter, Gantt anticipates the horrific destruction inevitable in a Civil War.

Everything is in a most unsettled state & the prospect is black enough politically speaking but not nearly so black as the alarmists picture. If the border states stand firm refusing to be ordered into the mad vortex of secession the troubles now distracting us will be composed. If the whole South secedes our condition will be terrible [?]. A Southern league means civil war. . . . All the fierce and angry passions of the country will be roused if a southern league is formed and a war will ensue from which mutual destruction will flow. But the consequence very bad for the north will be worse for the south and among the certain results will be the overthrow of the institutions which the south particularly cherishes. It is because the Union is the great protector of the south from the unspeakable evils which will flow from such a struggle that I trust all true friends of the south will hold fast to it through storm and through sunshine. But I am saying more than you will have patience to read. With my kindest regards to Mrs. Campbell and to your brother.

I am Very Sincerely your friend Thos. T. Gantt

Robert Campbell papers, Campbell House Museum.

JAMES BROADHEAD

Virginia native James Overton Broadhead was a member of the Committee of Safety, which was organized to cooperate with the military and national government to keep Missouri in the Union. Broadhead was unswervingly loyal to the Union. Baptist minister Galusha Anderson described him as an "ardent patriot without fanaticism." Broadhead had served in the Missouri State Legislature in the 1840s and 1850s and moved to St. Louis in 1859.

In his account of the committee's activities in the spring of 1861, he writes of adopted St. Louisan, Congressman-elect Frank Blair, son of Washington powerhouse Preston Blair and brother of Lincoln's postmaster general, St. Louisan Montgomery Blair. Lincoln worked through Frank Blair to keep St. Louis with the Union. Frank Blair publicized a meeting at Washington Hall, located on the riverfront, on January 11 to consolidate the city's Unionist support. Twelve hundred attended the meeting and voted to organize a Central Union Club, with branches throughout the city and county, open to anyone believing in the primacy of the Union. They vested Blair with authority to appoint the Committee of Safety, to act in behalf of the Unconditional Unionists.

Broadhead refers to the major political movements of the day including the Unconditional Unionists, who were dedicated to preserving the Union, and the Conditional Unionists, who were for the Union if slavery were allowed to continue. He mentions activities of the Minute Men, or secessionist volunteers. Broadhead tells of people being condemned as "Black Republicans," a derisive term for supporters of Lincoln and of supporters of racial equality.

In this personal account of the committee in the spring of 1861, Broadhead mentions members of the Filley family. Oliver D. Filley, mayor of St. Louis from 1858 to 1861, headed the movement to arouse and consolidate Union sentiment and acted as the committee's chairman. A New Englander, he was the eldest son of the Filley family in St. Louis. A tinner, he arrived in St. Louis in 1833 and found work in a stove manufacturing shop. He bought out the company and went into partnership with his brother, Giles Filley. He also refers to Turners, or members of Turnvereins.

As the last surviving member of the Committee of Safety, Broadhead wrote his account about 1897. The following passages, which include volatile scenes, begin with noting that the committee hired a detective force, headed by a former chief of police.

The detective force was paid for their services, and they were to report from time to time any material facts which came to their knowledge touching the movements of the Secessionists. For a long time, and during this most exciting period, they [the committee] met every night at Turner's Hall, corner of 10th and Walnut. Blair, of course, was frequently absent, as he was then a member elect of Congress.

I am now, and have been for many years, the only survivor of that Committee. The meeting at Washington Hall on the night of the 11th of January, at which the Republican party was, for the time being, dissolved and merged into the Union party, was the initial step in a series of movements which was finally instrumental in securing the State of Missouri to the Union. . . . The secessionists throughout the State, under the lead of the Governor and Lieutenant Governor, Jackson and Reynolds, . . . and others, were active, aggressive and prescriptive. No public meeting was held during that time in St. Louis, except the two of the 11th and 12th of January, at which the supporters of Mr. Lincoln were not denounced as Black Republicans; declaring at one of their meetings, that "they would do what they could to remove from St. Louis the stigma of being an anti-slavery Black Republican county, hostile to the institutions of the State of Missouri." They seemed more intent upon crushing out or driving from the State, as they frequently threatened to do, the small band of Republicans who had voted for Mr. Lincoln, than of preserving the Union. Indeed, they were not for preserving the Union, but for joining the revolutionary cohorts which afterwards commenced the war against the Federal Government.

It was at a meeting at Washington Hall on the 7th of January, that the minute men were organized. Charles McLaren was President of the meeting. Prior to, or shortly after the meeting of the Republicans at Washington Hall on January 11th, . . . there had been a meeting of prominent Union men at the counting room of A.D. Filley on Main Street, to consider what should be done in the way of personal protection against the threats and domineering spirit of the secessionists, for there is no doubt that threats had been made to drive out of the city the prominent Unconditional Union men from the central and northern portion of the city where they were in the minority. Their lives were threatened, and rumors were circulated that the State guards intended to take possession of the Arsenal, and so it was determined at this meeting that the Union men should arm themselves with such weapons as they could procure; a sum of money was raised for the purpose, and all the Sharp's Rifles and other weapons of the kind were purchased from Woodward, who kept a gun store on Main Street. Mr. Giles Filley tells me that he bought 50 Sharp's Rifles with which he armed the men in his factory, and he says his men were two nights under arms owing to a rumor that the State guards under General Frost intended to make an effort to take the Arsenal.

At this time, Mr. Samuel T. Glover had his office at the corner of Fourth and Olive. On one occasion, Sam Gaty, a client of his and a strong secessionist, came into the office and seeing a gun there asked Mr. Glover what he was doing with a gun in his office. Mr. Glover replied: "You d--d secessionists don't expect to drive the Union men out of the city do you?"

No one who was not a close observer of current events at that day can form any conception of the prescriptive and malignant spirit which existed among the secessionists throughout the State. As an evidence, it may be stated that in the county of St. Charles, Landfield, a school teacher, was ordered to leave the county because he had voted for Mr. Lincoln and advocated the doctrines of the Republican party. He asked for a hearing, and he was tried by a committee of 28 of the most prominent citizens of the county, among whom were Dr. McElhaney, Joseph Alexander, B.A. Alderson, and others of equally high standing . . .

At the meeting held in A.D. Filley's office, provision was also made for organizing a body, or bodies, of men who should serve in the work of mutual protection, and accordingly, such companies were formed in various parts of the city.

Sixteen companies were thus formed, composed of about 1400 men. Between that time and the 15th of February 1861, they were drilled in different parts of the City. The writer belonged to a company which was drilled in a large room in the upper part of Winklemeir's Brewery on Market Street. Mr. Blair was President of the organization, but they all acted in harmony with the Committee of Safety.

During the time of organizing the companies of Union Guards, Gov. Yates of Illinois, forwarded 200 muskets for the use of the St. Louis Union men, which were shipped to Mr. Giles F. Filley, care of Woodward & Co. hardware dealers. They then were sent to Turner's Hall in a beer barrel under cover of some beer barrels, and there distributed to reliable Union men. About this time, a subscription was raised in support of the Union case. This matter was placed in the hands of Samuel R. Filley and E.W. Fox; and from St. Louis and the East, the sum of about $30,000 was raised.

St. Louis During the Civil War, c. 1897, Broadhead papers, Missouri History Museum Archives, 28-31.

CAPTAIN JAMES EADS

During February 1861, meetings were held across the city. An enthusiastic crowd attended a meeting at Ruedi's Beer Garden on Second Street on February 13. According to the *Daily Missouri Democrat* of the following day, "The sentiment or devotion to the flag of freedom repeatedly awoke the heartiest plaudits."

On that same night, the Citizens Union Meeting was held at Soulard Market. The meeting was conducted in a room in the upper story of the market building. The big crowd representing the workingmen of the Second Ward filled the room that measured 120 feet long by 40 feet wide. A large American flag with thirty-four stars was suspended over the stand.

Self-taught river engineer James Eads was selected as chairman of the meeting. After thanking the audience for the honor, he talked about the preponderance of foreign born, mostly Germans, supporting the Union cause. He celebrated their patriotism.

When I cast my eyes over this large and intelligent mass of my countrymen, and see among them so many of our adopted citizens rallying to the standard of the republic—and when I reflect that among all those who are now plotting their country's ruin there is not one of foreign birth enrolled within their ranks, I feel alternate emotions of gratitude and shame. Gratitude to them for their devotion to the flag of their country, and shame to think that to none but Americans—native-born Americans—belongs the dishonor of humiliating that emblem of the nation's glory. I thank God that our adopted citizens have, by an unanimous sentiment of devotion to the Union, been enabled to administer, by their example, a rebuke at once so severe and so well merited to those ungrateful men who are laboring to defile that banner under whose protecting shade they first inhaled the sacred air of liberty. The united voice of nine tenths of the American born people of this land, uttered in execration of this Southern revolution, would not carry with it one half the moral force of the rebuke which our adopted citizen are giving to it by their unanimous devotion to the Constitution.

This Union has given to our people prosperity at home and respect abroad. It has secured to us free speech, free thought, and a free press. It has fostered the arts and sciences, encouraged manufactures, promoted virtues, administered impartial justice, and has secured to us the rights to worship the Most High according to the dictates of our own consciences. Under its beneficent influence, Missouri has grown in forty years to be a mighty empire in herself, and our own St. Louis, of which we are justly proud, is now the queen city of the Union.

Eads then questioned what secession could offer Missourians and stated that joining the South would be a poor trade compared to staying in the Union. He then warned secessionists.

Madmen and fools of the South! Go on in your insane endeavor to make slaves more secure by destroying the Union which now protects them; but be assured that no fanatical abolitionist of the North can desire a speedier solution of the slavery question than the destruction of this government will precipitate upon the South. . . .

Eads concluded his speech with this rallying call.

Were all sense of justice, generosity and good will fled from the human heart; were not patriotism; national honor and pride of country implanted in the bosom of every true American, then might we hang our heads in hopeless despair; but whilst all these, and a thousand others conspire to cheer us, let us swear by Heaven that this Union must and shall be preserved.

Daily Missouri Democrat, *February 14, 1861, St. Louis Public Library.*

JULIUS ROMBAUER

After a thirty-four-hour Confederate bombardment, federal Fort Sumter was surrendered to the Confederates on April 14. The following day, on April 15, Lincoln called for 75,000 men to volunteer. St. Louisan Robert Julius Rombauer, who answered that call, had fled to America and then settled in St. Louis after the failed Hungarian Revolution of 1848. On May 7, 1861, Lieutenant-Colonel Rombauer was appointed second-in-command of the First Regiment, United States Reserve Corps in St. Louis, Missouri. His regiment was part of the federal force to surround and capture the pro-Confederate Missouri State Guard at Camp Jackson at Grand and Lindell boulevards, then on the fringes of St. Louis.

Even though the governor of Missouri and the State Militia sided with the secessionists, when Lincoln called for 75,000 men, St. Louis was prepared. Rombauer stated, "The rising of [more than] 10,000 St. Louis loyalists is one of the most striking demonstrations of popular power, based on correct principles and wielded with the momentum of a systematic organization."

In 1909, his book, *The Union Cause in St. Louis in 1861: An Historical Sketch*, was published. To produce this document, Rombauer studied then-disintegrating records. He toiled to create a concise summary of names of the Missourians who answered Lincoln's call.

Rombauer noted the nationality of the more than ten thousand men who enlisted for three months' service. He wrote that 80 percent were German, 12 percent were American, and 8 percent were French, Irish, Bohemian, and other nationalities. Three Turner (members of Turnvereins) companies had long been ready to defend the Union. Frank Blair was the natural leader of the First Volunteer Regiment. Nearly 50 percent of that regiment were German, over 42 percent American and French, and about 8 percent Irish. In these passages, Rombauer also noted the sites where the Home Guard drilled, and he commented on the position of local churches.

The aggregation of the first Companies of the First Volunteer Regiment was accomplished in and by the St. Louis Turn Verein, with some members from kindred Societies and sympathetic associates. Members of the Union Clubs, former State Militia officers and men, with a large proportion of Americans, formed the other Companies, of which one was manned almost entirely by loyal Irishmen. . . . The First Regiment Volunteer Infantry of Missouri organized April 27, 1861, by electing Francis P. Blair Colonel.

The leading spirit in the Second Missouri Volunteer Regiment was Henry Boernstein, editor of the "Anzeiger des Westerns," an energetic, able man of radical views and a gifted writer. Being a leader in political, social and theatrical enterprises he became popular and influential, chiefly among citizens of German descent. Henry Boernstein was born November 4, 1805, in Hamburg, educated at the University of Lemberg in Galicia, joined the Austrian army and married in Buda, Hungary. He followed theatrical and journalistic pursuits at Paris, France, where he took an active part in the revolution of 1848. Emigrating to this country, he first practiced medicine, afterwards became editor and proprietor of the "Anzeiger des Westens," at that time a radical Republican paper. Boernstein was the founder of the "Free Mens' Rationalistic Society," promoted theatre enterprises and progressive institutions and took a very active part in politics. Peter J. Osterhaus, who became one of the best Generals of the Union Army, and Colonel Fred Schaefer, who fell at the battle of Murfreesboro, were members of this Regiment. Drilling was going on long before the President's call, among other places, at the house of Professor A. Hammer, an eminent surgeon, where the students of the Humboldt Institute assembled and were instructed by P. J. Osterhaus in anticipation of coming events. At one such evening an alarm was heard and Dr. Hammer excitedly rushed for his revolver, which the cool-headed Osterhaus quietly took from him. The house of Dr. Hammer stood on the ground of the present Anheuser-Busch Brewery, then in embryo state, and as that was almost within pistol shot of the Arsenal gate, the Doctor's excitement could be readily explained. A squad of about twenty students, to whom Lyon furnished muskets, held here an advanced guard. Osterhaus afterward aided to form the Second Volunteers, whose Rifle Battalion he commanded, which rendered eminent service at the battle of Wilson's Creek. Dr. A. Hammer aided the formation of the Fourth Volunteers, whose Lieutenant-Colonel he was; Dr. Joseph Spiegelhalter that of the Fifth Volunteers and other squads and their members, aided similarly in different organizations, according to the immediate need and convenience, as the spontaneous and elementary nature of the Union movement demanded. Rank and advancement was gained quick. The Private of one day was made Captain the next, and the Commander of a Battalion or Regiment the third or fourth day.

Francis Sigel, the most prominent organizer of the Third Regiment Volunteers, had an established reputation as a military man. As second in command of the revolutionary army at Baden in 1848, he gained the appreciation of his countrymen in a high degree; as a man of decided progressive republican views, possessed of a good military education, it was obvious that he should become a leader in military affairs. Sigel was Superinendent of the German Institute of Education, which enjoyed a very good reputation. The Second and Third Regiments were manned almost entirely by Germans.

The "Schwarze Jaeger," or Fourth Regiment Missouri Volunteers, had its origin in a hunting and rifle club of many years' standing. Its members were chiefly German immigrants, their leader in 1861 was Nicolaus Schuettner, a carpenter by trade, who made up for his lack of education by a most resolute patriotism and the earnestness of deep conviction. There were a few Americans in some of their Companies, and in one a great many Bohemians. The "Schwarze Jaeger" were always armed and being accustomed to the handling of rifles, having the practice and outfit of hunters, were in the first four months of 1861, and up to April 21, of more consequence than most other Union organizations, as they could be counted upon in the defense of the Asenal for immediate armed resistance. The original Schwaze Jaeger Society was largely composed of men who had been in military service in Europe. They assembled for gun and rifle practice and had social gatherings. They commenced to organize miltary Companies for field service early in 1861 at several points, such as Ruedi's Garden, South Third, Broadway near Park and Arsenal and Broadway, Jaegers' Garden and Wild Hunters.

When Captain Anthony Niederwieser planted the Union flag on the southeast corner of Broadway and Pine, right opposite the Minute Men's Secession ensign, Captain Schuettner, with a Company of about forty men from the original "Schwarze Jaeger," mounted guard for its protection.

The Fifth Regiment Missouri Volunteers was organized by electing C.E. Solomon Colonel. The first meetings of men for its organization were held on Park avenue and Seventh street and at Flora Garden. The members came chiefly from the Southern part of town, Carondelet and from St. Louis County. . . . The Regiment organized on May 18. . . .

The slower organization of this Regiment was owning to the fact that the first four Regiments had filled the Missouri quota under the President's call for 75,000 men, and the Fifth Volunteers muster in was only made legal after the President increased the Missouri quota to 10,000 men.

The political excitement carried its partisan fire also into the churches; the Catholic houses of worship were least affected because they were governed in the main by their highest capacities. The German churches were on the Union side, the majority of the American favored Secession; some had a divided congregation, while others had a decided Union membership and eminent preachers. Eliot and Galusha Anderson were animated apostles of truth and liberty, and did much to develop the Union cause among American religious people.

Robert Julius Rombauer, The Union Cause in St. Louis in 1861: An Historical Sketch *(St. Louis: Nixon-Jones Printing Company, 1909), 195-199. St. Louis Public Library.*

JAMES MCDONOUGH

CHIEF OF POLICE

While the environment threatened all, the situation for African-Americans in St. Louis, free or slave, was even more precarious. Notices from the chief of police, carried in the *Daily Missouri State Journal*, referred to passes, curfews, and licenses required for African-Americans to reside in the state.

Office of Chief of Police, St. Louis, April 5, 1861.
All negroes found in the street after the hour of ten o'clock, without a proper pass, will be arrested and brought before the Recorder.

—Jas. McDonough, Chief of Police

By order and direction of the President of the Police Commissioners of the city of St. Louis, I hereby notify all free negroes and mulattoes who have no license, or are not permitted by law to reside within this State, to leave the State forewith; and all such who may be found in the city of St. Louis after the expiration of five days from the date of this notice, will be arrested and dealt with according to the law.

—Jas. McDonough, Chief of Police
Daily Missouri State Journal, *April 29, 1861, Evening.* St. Louis Public Library.

JAMES McDONOUGH, CHIEF OF POLICE.

St. Louis Christian Advocate Describes the Atmosphere After Fort Sumter

Many newspaper articles from Civil War–era St. Louis read like personal columns. While relating facts, they were often filled with emotions and personal opinions. The *St. Louis Christian Advocate*, which sympathized with the South, carried an article on April 18, 1861, following the attack on Sumter, but before hostilities erupted in St. Louis.

It refers to the new police regulations that limited the operations of beer gardens. Since beer gardens were a popular gathering place for Republican German-Americans, this regulation disrupted the ability of German-Americans to organize support for the Union.

In this city the excitement is earnest and deep, but comparatively quiet. It is like "the calm that precedes the storm." No one knows what a day may bring forth. We hear that many rumors are afloat, but what they are, we are not prepared to say, not being in the secrets of any party.

The Arsenal is reported as being strengthened and fortified, as if the commandant there apprehended trouble, though we have heard of no threats made against it. The people are divided— some holding one way, some the other. We hope there may be no outbreak, no disorder.

The new police regulations seem to work well. Last Sunday, for the first time during years past, the liquor shops, beer gardens, Sunday theaters, &c., were closed. This is a great improvement on former times. Other improvements have been promised, and, we suppose, will be carried out.

At the beginning of this week, and indeed, during a few days previously, there was some excitement here, growing out of a report that the commandant at the Arsenal had been directed to distribute five or six thousand stand of arms among the Germans in the lower part of the city. The Democrat of Tuesday morning denied that the distribution was to be confined to the Germans, . . .

St. Louis Christian Advocate, *April 18, 1861.*

CAPTAIN ALBERT TRACY

Federal troops were mobilizing. Locally, supplies and men were transferred from Jefferson Barracks to the Arsenal in South City. The Arsenal, located at the south end of the Soulard neighborhood two miles south of downtown, had been established in 1826. Its stone walls warehoused sixty thousand muskets, forty-five tons of gunpowder, over one million cartridges, forty cannons, and machinery to repair and manufacture more arms. It was coveted by both the North and South.

Jefferson Barracks covered more than seventeen hundred acres then ten miles south of the city of St. Louis (now in South St. Louis County). Established in 1826, it was one of the most important military installations in U.S. history and the principal reserve depot for the Army of the West. It served as the site for the first infantry school in the United States.

Captain Albert Tracy, who unconditionally supported the Union, wrote in his journal about troops moving rifle powder from Jefferson Barracks to the Arsenal in St. Louis. His journal entry dated May 2 is filled with alarm about the casual attitude of the troops moving the dangerous, explosive materials.

Blair's Regiment of Missouri Volunteers, which has for a short time past garrisoned the Barracks below, marched up this evening, under an order from Lyon, to aid in, as well as cover, the removal of such portions of the rifle-powder stored here, and as can be placed in the Magazine at the Arsenal. Taking into consideration the perfectly wild and reckless manner in which barrels containing each one hundred pounds of the material in question, were tumbled about, and "toted" down-hill from the magazine buildings, and finally cast into a pile by the rail-track, it is nothing short of a mercy that no accident happened to induce an explosion. The very nails in the men's boots, streaked at points with the leakage from the barrels, might have caused ignition. I was also fain to suggest to Blair himself to put out the light of his cigar. Four hundred and odd barrels! More than forty thousand pounds of live rifle powder! And then there was the locomotive for the cars to bear away the dangerous explosive. It took position, after uncoupling, and during the loading up, just by the edge of the grove, beyond the upper portion of the magazine grounds, with sparks that drifted from the funnel as if it were upon a very errand of destruction,—threatening, any instant, the little black piles of powder that escaped here and there by the pint from the barrels. And when, too, the cars had been filled and closed, the locomotive must need to back down a quarter of a mile or more, over some ties in the road, which had been smouldering from chance sparks since yesterday,—as if for the last chance of a blow-up, by the sifting out of loose particles upon the red-hot glowing brands beneath. It seemed to me I felt as much relief with the second and final passage of that locomotive, with its attached burthen, away up towards Carondelet and the City, as if I had gotten safely through a battle. . . .

Ray W. Irwin, ed., "Missouri In Crisis: The Journal of Captain Albert Tracy, 1861, Part I," Missouri Historical Review (October 1956): 20-21.

WILLIAM TECUMSEH SHERMAN

West Point graduate, Ohio native, and brother of U.S. Senator John Sherman, William Tecumseh Sherman was the superintendent of the Louisiana Military Academy in Baton Rouge when the year 1861 began. When it was evident that Louisiana would join the seceding states, he resigned from his position. He and his family moved to St. Louis where he signed on as the president of a local streetcar company.

In his memoirs, Sherman noted the sites of his home and office in downtown St. Louis, the streetcar operations in Bremen (North St. Louis City), and the mansion turned into Confederate headquarters near the Old Courthouse. In these passages, he also referred to many of the city's political and military leaders and described the threatening environment.

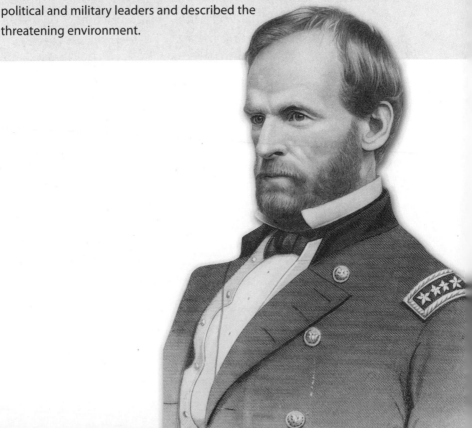

Mrs. Sherman and I gathered our family and effects together, started for St. Louis March 27th, where we rented of Mr. Lucas the house on Locust Street, between Tenth and Eleventh, and occupied it on the 1st of April. Charles Ewing [Sherman's brother-in-law] and John Hunter [Ewing's childhood friend] had formed a law-partnership in St. Louis, and agreed to board with us, taking rooms on the third floor. In the latter part of March, I was duly elected president of the Fifth Street Railroad, and entered on the discharge of my duties April 1, 1861. We had a central office on the corner of Fifth and Locust, and also another up at the stables in Bremen. The road was well stocked and in full operation, and all I had to do was to watch the economical administration of existing affairs, which I endeavored to do with fidelity and zeal. But the whole air was full of wars and rumors of wars. The struggle was going on politically for the border States. Even in Missouri, which was a slave State, it was manifest that the Governor of the State, Claiborne Jackson, and all the leading politicians, were for the South in case of a war. The house on the northwest corner of Fifth and Pine was the rebel headquarters, where the rebel flag was hung publicly, and the crowds about the Planters' House were all more or less rebel. There was also a camp in Lindell's Grove, at the end of Olive Street, under command of General D.M. Frost, a Northern man, a graduate of West Point, in open sympathy with the Southern leaders. This camp was nominally a State camp of instruction, but, beyond doubt, was in the interest of the Southern cause, designed to be used against the national authority in the event of the General Government's attempting to coerce the Southern Confederacy. General William S. Harney was in command of the Department of Missouri, and resided in his own house, on Fourth Street, below Market; and there were five or six companies of United States troops in the arsenal, commanded by Captain N. Lyon; throughout the city, there had been organized, almost exclusively out of the German part of the population, four or five regiments of "Home Guards," with which movement Frank Blair, B. Gratz Brown, John M. Schofield, Clinton

B. Fisk, and others, were most active on the part of the national authorities. Frank Blair's brother Montgomery was in the cabinet of Mr. Lincoln at Washington, and to him seemed committed the general management of affairs in Missouri.

The newspapers fanned the public excitement to the highest pitch, and threats of attacking the arsenal on the one hand, and the mob of d----d rebels in Camp Jackson on the other, were bandied about. I tried my best to keep out of the current, and only talked freely with a few men; among them Colonel John O'Fallon, a wealthy gentleman who resided above St. Louis. He daily came down to my office in Bremen, and we walked up and down the pavement by the hour, deploring the sad condition of our country, and the seeming drift toward dissolution and anarchy. I used also to go down to the arsenal occasionally to see Lyon, Totten, and other of my army acquaintance, and was glad to see them making preparations to defend their post, if not to assume the offensive.

Sherman then described St. Louis following the Confederate attack on Fort Sumter. The atmosphere filled with intrigue and late-night meetings.

Later in that month, after the capture of Fort Sumter by the Confederate authorities, a Dr. Cornyn came to our house on Locust Street, one night after I had gone to bed, and told me he had been sent by Frank Blair, who was not well and wanted to see me that night at his house. I dressed and walked over to his house on Washington Avenue, near Fourteenth, and found there, in the front-room, several gentlemen, among whom I recall Henry T. Blow. Blair was in the back-room, closeted with some gentleman, who soon left, and I was called in. He there told me that the Government was mistrustful of General Harney, that a change in the command of the department was to be made; that he held it in his power to appoint a brigadier-general, and put him in command of the department, and he offered me the place. . . . [Sherman told Blair] must decline his offer, however tempting and complimentary.

Through political maneuvering, Captain Nathaniel Lyon assumed control of the St. Louis Arsenal and its troops. The Connecticut native and West Point graduate was known for his fiery temper. While serving in Kansas, he had watched as tensions between pro-slavery and free-soil advocates often erupted into violence.

The Arsenal was framed by the river on the east and a ten-foot-high stone wall on the landsides. It included a foundry, workshops, warehouses, and four stone barracks.

Thousands of untrained volunteers from the city's German community helped defend the Arsenal.

With his children, Sherman visited the prized Arsenal and saw its commander, General Nathaniel Lyon.

I remember going to the arsenal on the 9th of May, taking my children with me in the street-cars. Within the arsenal wall were drawn up in parallel lines four regiments of the "Home Guards," and I saw men distributing cartridges to the boxes. I also saw General Lyon running about with his hair in the wind, his pockets full of papers, wild and irregular, but I knew him to be a man of vehement purpose and of determined action. I saw of course that it meant business, but whether for defense or offense I did not know.

Governor Claiborne Jackson and his Confederate allies wanted control of the federal Arsenal. The Confederate sympathizing State Militia was organized and equipped. Brigadier General Daniel Frost, who was secretly working for Governor Jackson, commanded two St. Louis units. The units numbered eight hundred uniformed men, and their goal was to take the Arsenal. They set up Camp Jackson west of downtown on park-like grounds framed by Olive Street, Compton Avenue, Laclede Avenue, and Grand Boulevard.

Threats and plans of the militia to attack the Arsenal were reported. Since the Arsenal site was vulnerable, on ground sloping to the Mississippi River and below a nearby hill, Lyon had secretly shipped most of the weapons to safety in Illinois.

On May 10, Lyon and his fellow Union officers lead mostly German volunteers in a pre-emptive movement against Camp Jackson. Seven thousand soldiers marched west from the heart of downtown on Laclede Avenue, Pine Street, Market Street, Olive Street, Morgan Street, and Clark Avenue, surrounded Camp Jackson, and accepted the surrender of the Confederate militia's commander, General Frost.

As the inexperienced Union troops marched the prisoners back to the Arsenal, through the city streets, angry Confederate sympathizers hurled rocks and screamed.

Sherman described his own activities and encounters with people on the morning of May 10, 1861, as Union troops and volunteers moved on the Confederate Camp Jackson.

I went up to the railroad-office in Bremen, as usual, and heard at every corner of the streets that the "Dutch" were moving on Camp Jackson. People were barricading their houses, and men were running in that direction. I hurried through my business as quickly as I could, and got back to my house on Locust Street by twelve o'clock. Charles Ewing and Hunter were there, and insisted on going out to the camp to see "the fun." I tried to dissuade them, saying that in case of conflict the by-standers were more likely to be killed than the men engaged, but they would go. I felt as much interest as anybody else, but staid at home, took my little son Willie, who was about seven years old, and walked up and down the pavement in front of our house, listening for the sound of musketry or cannon in the direction of Camp Jackson. While so engaged Miss Eliza Deans, who lived opposite us, called me across the street, told me that her brother-in-law, Dr. Scott, was a surgeon in Frost's camp, and she was dreadfully afraid he would be killed. I reasoned with her that General Lyon was a regular officer; that if he had gone out, as reported, to Camp Jackson, he would take with him such a force as would make resistance impossible; but she would not be comforted, saying that the camp was made up of the young men from the first and best families of St. Louis, and that they were proud, and would fight. I explained that young men of the best families did not like to be killed better than ordinary people. Edging gradually up the street, I was in Olive Street just about Twelfth, when I saw a man running from the direction of Camp Jackson at full speed, calling, as he went, "They've surrendered, they've surrendered!" So I turned back and rang the bell at Mrs. Deans's. Eliza came to the door, and I explained what I had heard; but she angrily slammed the door in my face! Evidently she was disappointed to find she was mistaken in her estimate of the rash courage of the best families.

The first action Sherman witnessed in the Civil War was as a civilian, in the streets of St. Louis, on May 10. It appeared that hostilities had been averted, and Sherman walked—with his seven year-old son Willie at his side—toward the troops. He watched as Confederate St. Louisans taunted German St. Louisans in Union volunteer uniforms and gunfire erupted. His young brother-in-law threw young Willie to the ground and then Sherman threw himself to the ground as bullets cut the leaves above their heads.

The supporters of secession derisively called the Germans the "damned Dutch." They had mispronounced the term "*Deutsch*," or German, as "Dutch."

I again turned in the direction of Camp Jackson, my boy Willie with me still. At the head of Olive Street, abreast of Lindell's Grove, I found Frank Blair's regiment in the street, with ranks opened, and the Camp Jackson prisoners inside. A crowd of people was gathered around, calling to the prisoners by name, some hurrahing for Jeff Davis, and others encouraging the troops. Men, women, and children, were in the crowd. I passed along till I found myself inside the grove, where I met Charles Ewing and John Hunter, and we stood looking at the troops on the road, heading toward the city. A band of music was playing at the head, and the column made one or two ineffectual starts, but for some reason was halted. The battalion of regulars was abreast of me, of which Major Rufus Saxton was in command, and I gave him an evening paper, which I had bought of the newsboy on my way out. He was reading from it some piece of news sitting on his horse, when the column again began to move forward, and he resumed his place at the head of his command. At that part of the road, or street, was an embankment about eight feet high, and a drunken fellow tried to pass over it to the people opposite. One of the regular sergeant file-closers ordered him back, but he attempted to pass through the ranks, when the sergeant barred his progress with his musket "a-port." The drunken man seized his musket, when the sergeant threw him off with violence, and he rolled over and over down the bank. By the time this man had picked himself up and got his hat, which had fallen off, and had again mounted the embankment, the regulars had passed, and the head of Osterhaus's regiment of Home Guards had come up. The man had in his hand a small pistol, which he fired off, and I heard that the ball had struck the leg of one of Osterhaus's staff; the regiment stopped; there was a moment of confusion, when the soldiers of that regiment began to fire over our heads in the grove. I heard the balls cutting the leaves above our heads, and saw several men and women running in all directions, some of whom were wounded. Of course there was a general stampede. Charles Ewing threw Willie on the ground and covered him with his body. Hunter ran behind the hill, and I also threw myself on the ground. The fire ran back from the head of the regiment toward its rear, and as I saw the men reloading their pieces, I jerked Willie up, ran back with him into the gulley which covered us, lay there until I saw that the fire had ceased, and that the column was again moving on, when I took up Willie and started back for home round by way of Market Street. . . . The great mass of the people on that occasion were simply curious spectators, though men were sprinkled through the crowd calling out, "Hurrah for Jeff Davis!" and others were particularly abusive of the "damned Dutch." Lyon posted a guard in charge of the vacant camp, and marched his prisoners down to the arsenal; some were paroled, and others held, till afterward they were regularly exchanged.

Accounts of civilian casualties varied. Twenty-eight civilian fatalities were reported. Undoubtedly, many more were wounded, some mortally, and were carried to nearby homes. Captain Constantin Blandowski, a Polish patriot who became an American patriot, was reported as the first person wounded in the conflict. Later in the month, Blandowski died of the wounds he received while defending his adopted flag of the United States of America.

William Tecumseh Sherman, Memoirs of General W. T. Sherman, By Himself, *Vol. I (New York: D. Appleton and Company, 1875), 168, 171-174.*

SARAH FULL HILL

When she was twelve, English-born Sarah Jane Full emigrated to America with her parents and settled in St. Louis. In 1858, she married Eben Marvin Hill (referred to here as E. M.), a Vermont native. They supported the Union, and Eben became an officer in the Union's Corps of Engineers.

In these passages from her memoirs, Sarah Hill recalled their circumstances before the war, hearing the news of Fort Sumter, and the threatening atmosphere on the streets following the Battle of Camp Jackson.

We were living in St. Louis at that time, not far from the old Fair Ground, in a little cottage which was our own home. We had our baby boy and E.M. was connected with my father in a large construction and building business which was quite successful. Life looked very fair and bright to us, for we were young, healthy and strong and were prospering.

She wrote that after Abraham Lincoln's election in November 1860, "the cauldron of rebellion in the South was seething," and many believed Lincoln would never be inaugurated. Then she remembered hearing the news of Fort Sumter.

One evening in April, E.M. came home looking very pale and as though he had received a great shock. He dropped into a chair and appeared so unlike himself I was alarmed and begged to know what the trouble was.

"I fear it is war," he said, "for South Carolina has fired on the flag and it cannot go unnoticed. The South has been preparing for this many months, and this is the pretext for war, while the North is not ready and never has believed this thing would come."

There was no dinner partaken by us that night for we realized what the consequences might be, and living in a border state, which was even then trying to secede, the conflict would probably be fierce and sanguinary.

Wild rumors were circulating. Uncertainty and fear reigned. Eben Marvin Hill cautioned his wife to stay close to home and to say little on current events. Sarah believed that her husband's and father's support of the Union was known and was resented by "the Southern element." She described an incident that occurred the day after the Battle of Camp Jackson, as her husband traveled from her parents' home to her home.

The following day E.M. had a narrow escape. Mother was sending me a small basket of home cooking by him, which she usually did on baking day. After leaving the streetcar, there was quite a distance to walk before reaching our house, part of the way across a deserted brick yard. E.M. was hastening across this when a couple of men stepped out from behind a brick kiln and attacked him, saying, "Now, you bloody Union man, we are going to clean you out and all others like you." E.M. did not stand on the order of his going, but sprinted away from there lively, the two men in pursuit. Finally they fired on him two or three times and he thought he was hit. He soon reached a street where there were houses and they did not follow. He reached home white and breathless, and when we unpacked the basket we found where a bullet had gone through it and through a package of cookies inside.

Sarah Jane Full Hill, edited by Mark M. Krug, Mrs. Hill's Journal—Civil War Reminiscences *(Chicago: Lakeside Press, 1980), 4-5, 14-17.*

Newspapers Debate Camp Jackson

s the weeks passed, debate raged over the violence on Olive Street that had followed the surrender of Camp Jackson. Both sides held radically different interpretations of what had transpired. And each inflamed the other. Partisan journalists and clergy carried on angry debates in the newspapers.

On May 22, the *Central Christian Advocate* described the fact that more secessionists had not been killed in the Battle of Camp Jackson as "An Act of Mercy." Editor of the *Central Christian Advocate*, the Reverend Charles Elliott DD, had helped draw a plan for separation of the Methodists in the South from Methodists in the North in 1844.

Friday, May 10, 1861, will be a second fourth of July in St. Louis, and all Missouri, for generations to come. On that day the rebel army were taken prisoners, without shedding a drop of human blood. When the rebel mob of secessionists attacked the United States army, shot down the military representatives of the supreme powers of the Union, and aimed at a rescue of traitors from the arrest of justice; the slight response of killing only some thirty of the assailants, was an act of Mercy.

The *St. Louis Christian Advocate*, a Southern Methodist publication edited by the Reverend David R. McAnally, responded on May 30, 1861.

"An act of Mercy!" The shooting down in cold blood of unoffending and defenceless men, women and children "an act of mercy!!" The staining the earth with human gore; the mangling of human bodies; the bereaving of wives of their husbands, mothers of their sons, fathers of their daughters, the desolating of quiet homes, and the crushing of bleeding hearts "an act of mercy!!!" Mercy to whom? To the bereaved parents? To the orphaned children? The weeping and heart-broken widows, or whom? Who calls the "killing of only some thirty" "an act of mercy!"

St. Louis Christian Advocate, *May 30, 1861.*

STATE MILITIA MEN

W ithin weeks, many of the State Militia men who had been at Camp Jackson reassembled, in open support of the Confederacy, at Camp Frost in Jefferson City. In their new camp, Private Joe Leddy composed a thirteen-verse song about Camp Jackson. The lyrics derisively refer to the German-Americans volunteering for the Union as "Hessians" or the "Dutch." The lyrics, set to the then-popular tune, "Happy Land of Canaan," included the following verses.

THE INVASION OF CAMP JACKSON BY THE HESSIANS

It was on the tenth of May
Kellys' men were all away
When the Dutch surrounded Camp Jackson
Led by Lyons the bear
And Boernstein & Blair
To drive us from the Happy Land of Canaan

chorus

Oh ah. The time for our triumph is coming
We will yet see the time
When all of us will shine
And drive the Dutch from our happy land of Canaan.

Lyons came into the Camp
With such a pompous tramp
And said Frost you will have to surrender
one half hour I'll give
That's if you want to live
To get out of this happy land of Canaan

The filthy dirty hogs.
Pounded upon our boys like dogs
And after taking all our ammunition
In double quick time,
They marched us into time
To march from our happy land of Canaan

The people gave three cheers
For Davis' volunteers
Which raised the Hessians indignation
They fired upon our Brothers
Killing sisters, wives and mothers
And took us from the happy land of Canaan

And now I'll take my rhyme
Way back to olden time
When our country was invaded by the Britons
But freedoms noble son
our own George Washington
Drove them far from this happy
land of Canaan

Missouri History Museum Archives.

DANIEL G. TAYLOR
MAYOR OF THE CITY OF ST. LOUIS

Fear and uncertainty permeated every aspect of life in St. Louis. Even the ordinary work of the day held a unique significance. Workers wondered if each task might be the last before violence erupted in any neighborhood, at any business, at any office. The biannual mayor's message, which was accompanied by reports of department heads, was filled with apprehension. The message was presented to the councilmen only three days after the Battle of Camp Jackson.

Mayor's Office, May 13, 1861
Gentlemen of the Board of Common Council:

The necessary devotion of my time for several days past to the discharge of pressing and imperative duties devolving upon me by the late disastrous occurrences in our city, has prevented that thorough investigation of the various departments of our municipal government which I had contemplated, . . .

For the first time in many years the Municipal Executive is deprived of the privilege of congratulating the legislative department upon the increasing prosperity and continued tranquility of our beloved city. The unhappy differences which distract our country and have involved our countrymen in a fratricidal war, have affected the peace, prosperity and happiness of our city in a very especial and peculiar manner. Divided, as our people are, in their views and opinions of the questions in controversy, and each and all zealous and active in sustaining their respective positions, excitements of an extraordinary and deplorable character have arisen, and collisions have occurred, involving a loss of life unparalleled in our municipal history. The events of the past week are sufficiently and painfully familiar to all of you to render unnecessary any repetition here of the terrible story. . . . in the midst of the prevailing excitement, with conflicting rumors and statements unsifted and undetermined, it would be unsafe to pronounce judgment as to the causes of these difficulties, or to point out with certainty the parties responsible for them; but as far as it shall be in the province or power of the City Government to arrive at a correct judgment, and to fix the due responsibility, it may be relied upon for the active and efficient exercise of all its functions and authority to that end. There is promise at present of a return of peace and order, and we ardently hope and trust that tranquility will be restored; and would call upon our citizens generally to refrain from any movement that may retard such a result.

But even in the midst of this general gloom, it is a source of gratification to know that the great mass of our people, surrounded by the most violent excitements, have remained loyal to the laws, and have cordially joined with the authorities in their efforts to maintain the high reputation of St. Louis as a law-abiding and order-loving city. In such measures as may be taken hereafter to restore the former peaceful relations, to enforce the laws and punish offenders, we may confidently rely upon the hearty and unanimous support and co-operation of our fellow-citizens.

Mayor's Message, Mayor's Office, May 13, 1861, St. Louis Public Library.

WILLIS PRITCHARD
WATER WORKS SUPERINTENDENT

Willis Pritchard, superintendent of Water Works, proudly reported that the department had laid nearly six miles of water pipe during the last fiscal year. He reported that the ice made in the reservoirs the previous winter was sold for $1,860. He noted that the reservoirs were in good condition, but required constant care and watchfulness. Then he concluded his report with a statement that reads like a prayer.

The proposed extension to our Waterworks cannot, of course, now be entertained. The unhappy condition of our country forbids anything but the sternest economy, and we can only hope the blessing of God Almighty will so direct the madness of the hour, that peace and prosperity will soon again smile over a united and happy people.

Respectfully submitted,
Willis R. Pritchard,
Superintendent of Water Works.

Water Works Office to Truman T. Homer, Esq., City Engineer, Mayor's Message, May 13, 1861, St. Louis Public Library.

St. Louis Christian Advocate

n the spring of 1861, the *St. Louis Christian Advocate* had greatly expanded its news section. On June 20, the paper carried this article describing how a tense atmosphere and an accident resulted in violence.

About 10 o'clock on Monday a most sad occurrence took place in the city, on Seventh street, near to Pine. The matter was summarily as follows:

A company of "Home Guards" was passing southward on Seventh street, and when near the room of the Recorder's Court, which is now held there, a shot was fired. It was an accidental discharge of a gun in the hands of one of the passing company, who, as he marched along, attempted to change a cap on his gun. This is the statement of several responsible persons who were close at hand, and saw the whole affair. Two or three well-known citizens, respectable and responsible as any, have asserted to us that they saw, and knew this to have been the fact. Immediately upon the firing of that accidental shot—which was done near the rear of the company—those of the Guards in front fired upon the crowd about the door and steps of the Court-room—fired into the Court-room, killing five citizens and badly wounding others. It has also been asserted that they killed or wounded several of their own comrades. This seems to have been the substance of the whole matter. Of course, it produced a most intense state of feeling among the citizens; and, for a time, the rush of excited people to and fro was terrible. It all occurred in full hearing, and partly in sight of our office. May we never witness the like again! It was a sad and shocking sight to see people, unarmed, unprotected and unsuspecting, shot down, and in an instant hurried, without warning, into the presence of their God.

LEONARD MATTHEWS

In many families, members were taking opposing sides. Leonard Matthews told his children how his father and his brother were in personal conflict over the state of the nation.

At this time, my father was trying to influence your Uncle Orville, who was then a midshipman at Annapolis, to resign from the Navy. I went to see him to try to counteract father's influence. My brother was loyal to the Government, saying he owed all he had to it, and intended to stand by the colors.

Matthews also recalled how he followed a common practice among the well-to-do. To personally avoid the draft, a man could pay a substitute. Matthews has a boastful tone as he explains how he brought down the price on buying a substitute, who would take his place, in harm's way.

Few, who have not had the experience, can tell or imagine conditions in families where there is a division of sentiment, as there always is along a border line. It became so intense in most instances that nearly all agreed among themselves to not mention the war at all. As I shall mention later, opinion was divided in our family, and partly for that reason, as well as because I had a beautiful young bride, I did not care to enter the armed conflict. Moreover, I was engaged in quite a large business, and it would have been very inconvenient for me to be drawn as a conscript. It was so with most business men, and substitutes were in demand. The so-called "substitute brokers," in collusion with officers in the Provost Marshal's department, got up a "corner" on substitutes, and were charging

$1,300 each for them. I avoided the brokers and advertised for a substitute. A very likely looking man, who had an honorable discharge from the regular army, applied. I asked him his price. He offered to go for one hundred dollars. I took him to the Provost Marshal's office, the old Berthold mansion, northwest corner Pine and Fifth streets. Dr. Julian Bates examined him, giving him a certificate of his fitness. When I applied to have him entered, I was sent from one office to another until my patience was gone. At last I went to the Provost Marshal and told him the trouble, with the remark if I could not enter the man here, I would go to higher authority. That saved the day and an officer was called to enter the man. The next day the papers published details of the affair and substitutes were obtainable at $100 instead of $1,300. My substitute corresponded with me for quite a while, but was either killed or became tired of writing.

Matthews, 62-65.

Robert Campbell

In letters to family members, Robert Campbell lamented how the outbreak of war had stifled the business environment. As a young man in the fur trade, Irish-born Campbell had worked with Jedediah Smith and Jim Bridger. Those adventures provided seed money, knowledge of the West, and associations that helped him build a network of businesses including dry goods, steamboats, banks, hotels, and real estate. As one of the wealthiest and most prominent entrepreneurs in St. Louis, his views of the economy are of special interest.

Campbell wrote to his niece, Margaret MacCulloch, on June 21, 1861,

The Robert Campbell House, courtesy the Campbell House Museum

. . . you have seen by the newspapers that our country is in a very deplorable condition, and no immediate prospect of a change business is almost suspended and rents greatly reduced and such. . . . To be the case until peace is returned. We are unfortunately in a condition to feel these changes less than most people as we are entirely out of debt. But we will be losers by the general depreciation of property in value and many who are indebted to us will not be able to pay for some time and other debts we will lose.

In a letter to his sister Ann, dated July 11, 1861, Campbell wrote,

The unfortunate condition of our country, now in a state of civil war, has completely paralyzed business & reduced rents to a degree that you can scarcely imagine and the probability is that I will not again for a long period if ever be able to make you another remittance, so you will have to husband this for future requirements. Hugh and I are both prudent in business and were therefore in a condition to meet the present emergencies, & I am happy to say that we are entirely out of debt, whilst many of our largest Mercantile Houses, both in St. Louis and in other sections of the country have failed, & I have seldom seen the prospect ahead so disastrous . . .

Robert Campbell Papers, Campbell House Museum.

Jessie Benton Fremont and General John C. Fremont

President Lincoln appointed Major General John C. Fremont as commander of the Western Military Department headquartered in St. Louis. In July, Fremont arrived in St. Louis, the hometown of his wife, Jessie Benton Fremont. She was the daughter of Missouri's influential Thomas Hart Benton, senator from 1821 to 1851. The senator and Jesse's political savvy had nurtured and spurred Fremont's political and military career. In 1856, he was the first Republican candidate for president of the United States.

When Fremont arrived in St. Louis, Union troops were based at Jefferson Barracks in South County and at the federal Arsenal in South City. Fremont established a camp for a regiment in Lafayette Park. He established Benton Barracks, named for his father-in-law, in North St. Louis. Benton Barracks could accommodate as many as 23,000 troops. He built ten earthen forts to defend the city's periphery.

In later life, Jesse supported them with her writing and publishing. In her book, *Souvenirs of My Time*, she recalled the mood in St. Louis during 1861. Her memoir makes vivid the deadly effect of shutting down river traffic on St. Louis commerce.

After this, and with all my happy memories of Saint Louis, think how hard it was to go back there to the feeling that met us in '61-- in the beginning of the war.

Everything was changed. There was no life on the river; the many steamboats were laid up at their wharves, their fires out, the singing, cheery crews gone—they, empty, swaying idly with the current. As we drove through the deserted streets we saw only closed shutters to warehouses and business places; the wheels and the horses' hoofs echoed loud and harsh as when one drives through the silent streets late in the night.

It was a hostile city and showed itself as such.

One gentle touch from the past softened this. My cousin herself was absent, and her family was in France, but she had written to her man-of-business to meet us and take us to her beautiful house where we had always felt at home. More than ever it seemed home now; the old butler, "uncle" Vincent, slow and gray, met and welcomed us, and from the wall smiled down in lasting youth and sweetness the young cousin who had known but seventeen happy and beloved years. Into that upper parlor where the closer family life had left its impress many troubled men came and found moments of rest. My cousin insisted we should use the house as we needed and it became the Headquarters of the Western Department. Standing in its own grounds with three streets bordering them, it was convenient for the review of the regiments which came pouring in from neighboring States. This is not the place to begin to tell of that mighty time. I only speak of the bit of home surviving the storm of war and giving us this ark with some household gods still left in it. There came the good Dorothea Dix, "given of Heaven" surely, for the help of the insane and prisoners, and now of the sick and wounded. And there came, every evening, after the army left, the good Admiral Foote, whose heart was sore that the work on the gunboats was stopped and precious time being given to the enemy to fortify. And there came General Sherman while waiting orders—out of favor because he had said not sixty nor ninety thousand men, nor two hundred thousand could end the war. And there General Grant was given his first command—and many and many a link of historical interest connects with that stately house which was now all that was left me of past days.

Though the old kind feeling crept out in side ways. Fine old linen, bottles of good wine, would be sent to me, without names, but with a line to say they were for the sick in hospital; and one said, 'Not sent to the wife of the Yankee General, but to the daughter of Mrs. Benton who always gave to all needing help.

Of all wars none can approach a civil war for distressing complications. I went there in July with brown hair, and came away in November gray.

Jesse Benton Fremont, Souvenirs of My Time *(Boston: Lothrop & Co, 1887), 166-68.*

On September 5, 1861, the *St. Louis Christian Advocate* published General Fremont's proclamation of martial law. In the seventh paragraph, Fremont created a political nightmare for Lincoln. He declared the property of anyone taking up arms against the United States as confiscated and their slaves as emancipated. With Lincoln still trying to lure the border states to the Union, Fremont's emancipation declaration advanced himself politically while it undermined the president's political strategy to keep the border states with the Union. His military leadership, along with his political maneuverings, lead to him being relieved of command.

PROCLAMATION.
Headquarters Western Dep't.
St. Louis, August 30, 1861

Circumstances, in my judgment of sufficient urgency, render it necessary that the Commanding General of this Department should assume the administrative powers of the State.

Its disorganized condition, the helplessness of the civil

authority, the total insecurity of life, and the devastation of property by bands of murderers and marauders who infest nearly every county in the State, and avail themselves of the public misfortunes and the vicinity of a hostile force to gratify private and neighborhood vengeance, and who find an enemy wherever they find plunder, finally demand the severest measures to repress the daily increasing crimes and outrages, which are driving off the inhabitants and ruining the State.

In this condition, the public safety and the success of our arms, require unity of purpose, without let or hindrance, to the prompt administration of affairs.

In order, therefore, to suppress disorders, to maintain as far as now practicable, the public peace, and to give security and protection to the persons and property of loyal citizens, I do hereby extend and declare established Martial Law throughout the State of Missouri.

The lines of the army of occupation in this State are, for the present, declared to extend from Leavenworth by way of the post of Jefferson City, Rolla and Ironton, to Cape Girardeau, on the Mississippi river.

All persons who shall be taken with arms in their hands, within these lines, shall be tried by Court Martial, and if found guilty, will be shot.

The property, real and personal, of all persons in the State of Missouri who shall take up arms against the United States, or who shall be directly proven to have taken active part with their enemies in the field, is declared to be confiscated to the public use, and their slaves, if any they have, are hereby declared free men.

All persons who shall be proven to have destroyed, after the publication of this order, railroad tracks, bridges, or telegraphs, shall suffer the extreme penalty of this law.

All persons engaged in treasonable corresondence, in giving or procuring aid to the enemies of the United States, in fomenting tumults, in disturbing the public tranquility by creating and circulating false reports or incendiary documents, are, in their own interest, warned that they are exposing themselves to sudden and severe punishment.

All persons who have been led away from their allegiance are required to return forthwith to their homes. Any such absence, without sufficient cause, will be held to be presumptive evidence against them.

The object of this declaration is to place in the hands of the military authorities the power to give instantaneous effect to existing laws, and to supply such deficiencies as the conditions of war demand. But it is not intended to suspend the ordinary tribunals of the country, where the law will be administered by the civil officers, in the usual manner and with their customary authority, while the same can be peaceably exercised.

The Commanding General will labor vigilantly for the public welfare, and in his efforts for their safety hopes to obtain not only the acquiescence, but the active support of the loyal people of the country.

J.C. Fremont,
Major General Commanding

St. Louis Christian Advocate, *September 5, 1861.*

SARAH FULL HILL

English immigrant and Union supporter Sarah Hill witnessed the lack of organization in the Union camps, inadequate clothing, poor food, and resulting illness. Her critique of General Fremont's leadership as commanding general of the Department of the West was severe. Though the abolitionists and Germans were loyal to him, Fremont was removed from command in November.

Sickness and death were playing sad havoc with our men lying in camp, neither properly clothed or fed by the Govenment. Gen. Fremont was in command of the Department of the West. He had been a girlish idol of mine from reading of his achievements as a Pathfinder, but my illusions vanished, for he was "weighed in the balance and found wanting." The "pomp and panoply of war" appealed more to him and his staff than the dire needs of his men in the field. E.M. wrote pitiful stories of the suffering of his men, not yet hardened to the exigency of camp life and the difficulty there was in cutting through the "red tape" to procure necessary supplies.

Hill described the Christmas season in St. Louis as "a dark and gloomy period. . . ." The whole nation had plunged into grief and mourning. And Sarah's own father had passed away. She spent most of her Christmas day at the bedside of a soldier brought in from one of the camps in Missouri, who was dying of typhoid fever.

He was from Iowa, had a good farm there, and a wife and three little girls, and was so anxious to get well for their sakes. I had nursed him most of the time since he was received in the hospital, and he clung to me for hope and courage, but this day he realized his condition and it was so pitiful to hear him call for his wife and babies. The end came toward evening after a hard day, and for his wife's sake, I did for her loved one what she would have liked done, for I did not know how soon I might be in a similar place.

Hill, 44, 59.

1862

"Suddenly, and almost without warning, a great calamity overtook our city as well as the whole country,"
—Daniel G. Taylor, Mayor of the City of St. Louis

By New Year's Day of 1862, the Civil War had transformed St. Louis. Commerce with the South had halted, stifling many aspects of the local economy and leaving the city unable to pay its bills. The city, however, was filled with energy as the economy and citizens had mobilized. Individual St. Louisans and the community were taking on new roles to preserve the Union.

The previous September, Unitarian minister and founder of Washington University, William Greenleaf Eliot, had proposed organizing civilian volunteers as the Western Sanitary Commission to work with Army Medical Corps. Starting with the mission of comforting the soldiers in camps and in hospitals, eventually the commission would supply medicine and surgical materials, doctors and nurses, and care for soldiers and refugees. These waves of refugees that would flee to St. Louis throughout the war included the families of Confederate soldiers, Union families driven from southwest Missouri by Rebel raiders, and freed slaves.

General Henry W. Halleck, who had replaced glamorous John C. Fremont the previous November, was faced with providing for the destitute refugees in St. Louis. The voluntary contributions by Union supporters helped greatly, but more was needed. Halleck authorized assessments— the hated General Orders No. 24—to fine Southern sympathizers for stated amounts of provisions, clothing, quarters, or money to fund relief for the suffering refugees. Irate St. Louisans against whom the levy was made protested the order. In February, however, an auction was conducted of goods seized from disloyal citizens, including pianos, carved rosewood furniture, Brussels carpeting, and fine library volumes.

While news from the eastern battles gave comfort and encouragement to secessionists in St. Louis, a former St. Louisan was giving local Unionists

cause to celebrate. Ulysses S. Grant, a native of Ohio and a West Point graduate, had married a local girl, Julia Dent. Grant had farmed on her father's
plantation in South County from 1854 to 1859. He had delivered firewood
in St. Louis. And for a short time, Grant lived on Barton Street in the Soulard
neighborhood. After reenlisting in the Federal Army in the spring of 1861,
he immediately demonstrated extraordinary leadership.

With combined Army and Navy assaults, Grant had captured Fort
Henry on the Tennessee River and Fort Donelson on the Cumberland River.
In April, he led the Union to a sobering victory in the Battle of Shiloh, the
most terrible battle yet seen on the American continent.

Major General John M. Schofield assumed command of the Union's
Department of Missouri, headquartered in St. Louis, on June 1. Within
weeks, all St. Louisans suspected of Confederate sympathies were ordered
to take the oath of allegiance to the United States government and to the
provisional government of the state. More families sympathizing with the
Confederacy left St. Louis. Others cringed and stayed as their anger grew
with repression.

Physically, the city kept changing. Buildings had been converted or
constructed to serve as hospitals for Union soldiers transported from western battles. River engineer James B. Eads had leased the Carondelet boatyards to build ironclads and mortar rafts. With the influx of workers at the
boatyards, the Carondelet community experienced a housing shortage.
John O'Fallon's 150 acres on Natural Bridge just west of North Grand was
now the site of Benton Barracks, with parade grounds, barracks, and hospitals. The barracks were luring entrepreneurs to open new restaurants,
photo studios, and taverns nearby. Fremont had ringed St. Louis with ten
defensive earthen forts.

It seems surreal that some day-to-day life continued virtually unaltered.
St. Louisans celebrated the completion of the dome on the Old Courthouse
at Fifth and Market streets. The enrollment at Saint Louis University, then
located on the 900 block of Washington Avenue, grew. During the 1860–
61 session which ended early because of the war, there were sixty-three
students from Southern states, mostly Louisiana. Predictably, during the
1861–62 session, the number of Southern students shrank to nine, several
of whom had remained from the preceding session only because they were

unable to communicate with their parents. Even without its Southern patronage, the session of 1862–63 began with an increased number of students registered—290.

Throughout 1862, life in St. Louis was cast against a horrifying backdrop of news of huge armies waging terrible battles.

In the Western Theatre of the war, Ulysses S. Grant continued to battle his way south, wresting control of railroads and the river systems. His campaign to cut the Confederacy in two, by controling the Mississippi River, moved toward and then hammered Vicksburg.

At the end of August, the Confederates were victorious at the Second Battle of Bull Run. The casualties were five times larger than the First Battle of Bull Run, which had shocked the Union.

In mid-September, Lee's attempt to invade the North was repelled at the deadly Battle of Antietam. Though Confederate losses were slightly less than the Union losses, Commanding General Robert E. Lee lost a quarter of his army.

On December 13, Union Army Major General Ambrose E. Burnside commanded over one hundred thousand men against Robert E. Lee, commanding over 72,000 men at Fredericksburg. Union generals ordered sixteen suicidal charges, across a four hundred-yard open plain, against a stone wall atop Marye's Heights.

Despite the lopsided Confederate victory, the Confederate Bredell family of the Lafayette Square neighborhood wept. Among the Confederates lost in the battle was their son, Captain Edward Bredell Jr., who used to play baseball in Lafayette Park.

SARAH FULL HILL

T he sewing machine was humming and the knitting needles clicking as Sarah, her mother, aunt, and sisters had become, like "Every loyal family," a soldiers' aid society. They sewed flannel shirts and comforters and knitted socks and mittens. After Sarah's father had passed away the extended family was living downtown. Sarah described her own volunteer efforts with war relief, and the growth of aid organizations.

The women's Soldiers' Aid Society had been organized and I offered my services which were gladly accepted and I was a busy woman those dark days of the winter of '61 and '62. A large vacant block of stores on Fifth and Chestnut streets was taken by the government for a hospital, and the store rooms on the ground floor were used as Headquarters of the Medical Corps. The three upper stories were used for the hospital. Later the Sanitary Commission occupied some of the empty lower rooms, and our Soldiers' Aid had two rooms on Chestnut Street. Afterward we became Auxiliary to the Sanitary Commission, but we started before that was organized.

At first there was little system or order in our work, each and every woman doing what she could, our main object being to help the sick soldiers, and we found plenty of work. Of course we were all giving our time and labor to the cause. The doctors and surgeons availed themselves of our help, and every day we women gathered at the rooms and scraped lint, tore and rolled bandages, knitted socks. We solicited donations of delicacies for the sick. Many boxes were packed and sent to the soldiers in the field hospitals. We were called on to assist the surgeons in their operations and to nurse the patients. There were no regular nurses then and volunteer nurses were scarce. There was much confusion and lack of system in the hospital work, I might almost say ignorance at first.

Later in her reminiscences, Hill wrote,

. . . we were frequently called on for nurses, for there was great lack of help in that line. Many days and nights of that winter I spent beside the beds of the sick, wounded and dying, assisting the surgeons in their gruesome work. They said I had good nerves and was not afraid of the sight of blood. The use of anesthetics was little known, and the doctors often called for me. They said I was quiet and efficient and obeyed orders and understood quickly.

Hill, 49–52.

GALUSHA ANDERSON

Baptist minister Galusha Anderson felt and witnessed the sense of enthusiasm stirred by Union troops singing as they marched to the riverfront. They were joining the command of Ulysses S. Grant, who would soon give the Unionists something to cheer about.

. . . by the order of General Halleck an army was rapidly gathered on the Mississippi above Columbus, Kentucky. General Grant had been fortunately ordered to organize, drill, and lead these troops. To join his command many soldiers were sent by Halleck from the encampments in and around St. Louis. I saw one morning a regiment of stalwart men from Indiana, marching with elastic step down Pine Street to the levee, their every movement instinct with exuberant life, and singing, in clear strong tones,

> "John Brown's body lies a-mould-
> ering in the grave;
> John Brown's body lies a-mould-
> ering in the grave;
> John Brown's body lies a-moulder-
> ing in the grave;
> His soul is marching on!
> Glory, halle-hallelujah! Glory,
> halle-hallelujah!
> Glory, halle-hallelujah!
> His soul is marching on."

That was about the middle of January, 1862. That

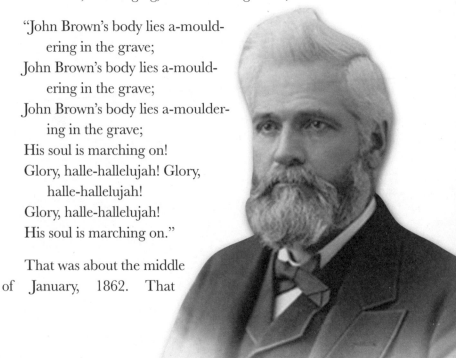

famous war song may have been sung before in our city, but this was the first time that I had heard it. It thrilled me through and through. That to me was an ecstatic moment. So it evidently was to the crowd that lined the street. They looked on as if entranced. Tears started in many eyes, and when the song, so prophetic of triumph, ended, the throng burst out into rapturous ringing cheers. And the patriots who sang those inspiring words were on their way to swell the ranks of Grant's army. Into the souls of all that heard them on that day came the assurance of victory.

As part of the federal campaign up the Cumberland and Tennessee rivers, Union troops commanded by Brigadier General Ulysses S. Grant conquered Fort Henry, an earthen fort on the Tennessee, on February 6. After capturing Fort Henry, Grant advanced cross-country to Fort Donelson. The fort's garrison, after failing in their all-out attack aimed at breaking through Grant's lines, surrendered on February 16. Ulysses S. Grant's victory ensured that Kentucky would stay in the Union and opened up Tennessee for a Northern advance along the Tennessee and Cumberland rivers.

In St. Louis, the news of these victories gave reason for celebration. Galusha Anderson described the jubilation in the streets of St. Louis that followed Grant's victories.

On the following day, February 17th, the news of the surrender came. More than fourteen thousand prisoners, with forty pieces of artillery, thousands of small arms and large quantities of commissary stores had been taken, and the Union troops occupied the fort. In spontaneous celebration of these glad tidings from all the encampments around our city came the roar of cannon; brass bands played "The Star-Spangled Banner' and "Yankee Doodle;" the Union Merchants Exchange laid aside all business and sang patriotic songs; large companies of Unionists, drawn together by some irresistible impulse, in the stores, in the market, on the streets, congratulated each other, laughed, clapped their hands and stamped their feet in glee. It was an hour of triumph; and the *Missouri Democrat* issued in hot haste an extra, heading its column with "Te Deum." It thus caught and expressed the sentiment then dominant in all loyal hearts, that of thanksgiving and praise to God, who presides over and directs the affairs of nations and in wisdom withholds or grants victories to armies. But our secession neighbors were mute. What gave us joy, gave them pain. At such times we always felt it to be sad that we were so divided.

The Union Army of the Mississippi and Army of the Ohio, 65,000 strong, battled the Confederate Army of the Mississippi numbering almost 45,000 men on April 6–7, 1862. The battle's 23,746 casualties stunned both the victorious North and the defeated South. Anderson called Shiloh "that field of carnage," and reported on the many dead and wounded.

The latter [the wounded] were sent up to St. Louis by boat-loads. They were carried on stretchers up through our streets to hospitals. The businessmen, merchants, clerks, manufacturers, bankers and artisans of various crafts helped bear along these ghastly burdens. Young men, the flower of the northwestern States, had been maimed, crippled, shot to pieces in defence of the Union. We were horror-stricken, and with a depth of emotion which we had not before felt, pledged to the defence of our government "our lives, our fortunes, and our sacred honor."

Waves of refugees fled into St. Louis throughout the war. These refugees included contrabands, or former slaves. By treating slaves as contraband of war, property neccessary for the Confederates to carry on the war, Union forces could legally free the enslaved. These refugees were particularly tragic. Anderson, however, found that though these freed slaves were horribly disadvantaged, they were more easily absorbed into the local economy than many of the white refugees.

The contrabands usually trudged into the city in groups, bearing in their hands or on their shoulders budgets, filled with old clothing or useless traps, their heads covered with dilapidated hats or caps, or, in the case of the women, wrapped about with red bandanas. Their garments were coarse, often tattered, and usually quite insufficient to shield them against the cold of winter. They wore shoes and boots of cowhide which in very many cases were nearly worn out, so that often their black toes protruded. But one cold, frosty, winter day a motley company of fugitives, men, women, and children, came marching in barefooted. We asked them how they came to be in such a wretched plight? They said that as they were going "long de road" out in the country, some "Confed sogers" seized them, set them on a bank by the roadside, and pulled off their shoes, and then told them just to run for their lives . . . compelling them to walk many miles with bare feet along frozen, snowy roads, the feet of the little children frost-bitten and bleeding.

. . . they were by no means as numerous as the white refugees; and while they were all illiterate, having been inured to labor they were usually ready to engage in any menial service. Those who had been trained in household work were at once employed by the best families of the city; while many field hands, that came to us in the winter, had to be cared for by the government and by private charity, until spring, when most of them found remunerative work in cleaning up yards, cultivating gardens, and on farms outside the city. Only a small contingent remained to tax our benevolence. Some of these were spiritless and thriftless; and some were crippled or sick. However, since the contrabands, taken as a whole, were ready to work, and were greatly delighted, for the first time in their lives, to work for wages, the problem of caring for them was comparatively an easy one.

Anderson, 244–45, 247, 262–63, 291.

Ernst Kargau

The writings of German-American journalist and essayist Ernst D. Kargau recall dissention, division, and changes in the local business community. Kargau was a native of the German province of Silesia. He had attended private schools and then business schools in Berlin before emigrating to America. From 1860 to 1888, he worked for St. Louis's German-American press. In 1893, the original German-language edition *St. Louis in Fruheren Jahren: Ein Gedenkbuch Fur Das Deutsche Element* was published.

The following excerpts, about the old Merchant's Exchange and about a popular German hotel on the riverfront, reflect how a year of war had created tumult and transformed St. Louis's economy.

The old Merchants Exchange on the east side of Main Street, between Market and Walnut, which at present looks insignificant, was in those days considered imposing and an ornament to the city. The bourse [stock exchange] was large enough for the business of the period, although on some days it was rather crowded. . . . At the outbreak of the Civil War there were some stormy scenes at the bourse. A part of the members sided with the secessionists for business reasons, or they held that the cotton barons had a perfect right to withdraw from the Union, if they so desired. The majority of the members were loyal to the Union. This difference of viewpoint led to a break. The members that sided with the North withdrew. They leased suitable rooms in a new building on North Third Street next to the post office. Here they opened a second bourse which they named Union Merchant Exchange. Those who sided with the South continued to support the Chamber of Commerce on Main Street. This break lasted for a whole year. The reunion took place in November, 1862. With it the old harmony was happily and permanently restored.

In the fifties and sixties the Rheinische Weinhalla (Rhenish Wine Hall) was regarded the best German hotel in the city. After Gustav Heinrichs had sold out to Louis Wolf the house became celebrated for its excellent kitchen, which reputation it has continued to maintain till this day, . . . Only a few rooms were rented by the month to some not-too-old bachelors. The demand of strangers made this restriction necessary. German merchants from Missouri and Illinois, who came here to do their buying, and representatives of eastern firms liked to lodge in this hotel because it was so close to Main Street which at that time was the main business street for almost all kinds of goods.

Kargau listed and described some of the regular German patrons at the hotel.

The years of the war provided a unique activity for the Rhenish Wine Hall. It was the favorite stopping place of officers of the Union army who came to St. Louis for a longer or shorter stay. Some of them who were on detached service, spent weeks and months there. Among these were Captain Indes, Major Poten, Major Hansen, Major Conrad and Lieutenant Grenzenbach. Also Prince Salm Salm, who had so faithfully remained with the unfortunate Archduke Emperor Maximilian in Mexico, was a guest here at that time. After the battle of Pea Ridge, in the spring of 1862, young Lieutenant Hermann Tuerk, (who at the beginning of the war had given up a position in one of the local business houses), was brought back here. An enemy bomb that had exploded close before him had destroyed his eyesight. The blind man received the best of care in Wolf's house for months. Later he was returned to his native city of Luebeck and to his parents. Through the efforts of local friends Congress allowed him a pension by a special legislative act.

Ernst D. Kargau, trans. by William G. Bek, ed. by Don Heinrich Tolzmann, St. Louis in Former Years: A Commemorative History of the German Element *(Columbia: University of Missouri Press, 1943), 4, 9-10.*

AN UNKNOWN SOLDIER

The reception given Iowa troops on the streets of St. Louis and images of camp life at Benton Barracks are included in diary entries made by an unknown soldier from Iowa. Though he used practically no punctuation, so his sentences often ran together, he painted vivid pictures of his journey to St. Louis and his time spent here. He began with the harrowing conditions on the riverboat headed for St. Louis.

The boat is crowded no place to sit & rest—The weather is hot and the water such a condition that it would soon kill the strongest man remaining in this situation any great length of time.

There is not a single accommodation not a single necessity furnished us, which is due the meanest human creatures—But a thousand men seemingly confined in a vast prison room enough on which to stand swaying to and fro as the vast throng wearies of its position.

But we are soldiers now and must expect everything requisite to man's comfort, convenience, and health taken from him.

We are greeted by the people upon each side of the river as we pass along.

On September 5, the troops arrived in St. Louis. The soldier recorded that while still on the boat north of St. Louis and while on the streets of the city, the ladies made the Iowa soldiers feel appreciated.

Passed Alton at 9 AM this morning. The Steamer S.B. Runyan passed us some 10 miles below There was a considerable number of ladies on board who gave us many manifestations of their patriotism which we of course returned.

We arrived at St. Louis at 10 AM & at 11 AM took up our line of march for the Barracks some 5 miles distant. We were greeted by the waving of flags and many expressions of encouragement from the ladies of almost every dwelling that we passed in going the entire length of the city. At one dwelling in particular I noticed a pair of pretty girls who seemed somewhat interested in us and I heard one remark to the other that the Iowa girls must have cried when our Regiment left for they were the best looking set of men she ever saw

Of course I do not vouch for the truth of her assertion (but I do know some of our fellows think themselves mighty good looking)

It was an exceedingly hot day and many of us unaccustomed to being bundled up in the amount of woolen goods we had on and the 50 lbs of a load we had to carry found to our satisfaction there was no fun soldiering and many a stout heart dropped by the way on account of his load. The Major and Chaplain done all they could to assist the weary and on that day many a poor fellow inwardly blessed them for their kindness in assisting to carry a part of their load.

Many of our boys availed themselves of the opportunity of taking a passage on the street cars

And at 1 O'clock PM the 19th passed into Benton Barracks.

Benton Barracks Mo Sept 6th 1862

This place is 5 miles from S Louis and is enclosed by a close high fence is one mile square and contains every variety of building necessary for containing a large number of troops. The place is nearly level the buildings all white washed and kept clean & in good order.

I understand there are 19,000 soldiers stationed here

Everything is conducted on the strict military discipline and it would be almost impossible for any to escape only two from each company can receive passes the same day to pass out

Our officers are not very hard upon us and our Drill of an hour each twice to day hardly gave us an appetite One or two of our boys are quite sick to day

The soldier described the field officers before relating that the regiment had experienced its first death, a soldier in Company G from Wappelo County. The next entry, on September 7, 1862, described life on a Sunday, beginning with declaring, "Sunday no drills to day."

Church at 10-30 AM at the camp Amphitheatre. We turned out in military order coats brushed boots polished faces washed and the corners of our handkerchiefs sticking out of our pocket . . .— Fell into two ranks form company—march we wended our way to church the brass buttons on our coats glistening in the sunshine and casting fantastic pictures over the ground while our officers in punkin rines and tinsel and scarlet guided us to the place of worship

Brother Murphy gave us a good sermon and if he did not feel proud of the 19th I did for we paid strick attention to all he had to say and joined in the hymn with right hearty good will

The 33d Missouri met with us their officer Col Fisk was introduced to our multitude to whom he made some scriptural remarks which were well received and we all thought he was a great and good man a praying fighting Christian who must make his mark go where he will

He told us he and his regiment would meet us again on next Sunday at that place—Short sighted mortals we are ere next Sunday we may be sunderd forever and it is very possible nay not almost but certain that the 19th Iowa & 33d Mo will never meet again as they have to day and mingle and commingle under the droppings of the sanctuary

Our first dress parade at Benton Barracks came off at 5 o'clock this evening

Diary of an Unknown Soldier, pages 1-3, Missouri History Museum Archives.

DANIEL G. TAYLOR

MAYOR OF THE CITY OF ST. LOUIS

After a year of war, St. Louis was unable to pay its bills because business languished due to the closing of the Mississippi and there was a loss of manpower as thousands of St. Louis's young men joined opposing armies. On May 20, 1862, Mayor Taylor issued a seven-page letter to the creditors of the city of St. Louis explaining the city's current circumstances.

Taylor, who was born in Cincinnati to immigrants from Scotland, had become a riverboat captain before setting up a home and wholesale business in St. Louis. He served as mayor of St. Louis from 1861 to 1863.

In the letter, the mayor wrote about the city's growth from 6,000 residents in 1836 to more than 160,000 citizens in 1860. He noted the city's physical expansion, including improvements to the harbor, waterworks, streets, and sewers. He wrote about the challenges the city had faced in the past, including the 1844 flood, the devastating fire of 1849, the ravaging cholera of 1849, and the crushing financial difficulties of 1857. And yet the municipality "always met our liabilities promptly as they became due. . . ." In these excerpts from the letter, he described the effects of the war on the St. Louis economy.

Suddenly, and almost without warning, a great calamity overtook our city as well as the whole country, and caused a disastrous change in our condition and prospects.

It is known to the world for more than a year past, that a rebellion of the most formidable character and dimensions has been raging in our country, and that civil war is devastating the southern half of it. It is known also, that our State (Missouri being on the border between the two contending parties to this deadly strife) has been since May, 1861, one of the principal scenes of this fratricidal war, and has suffered the fatal consequences of her unfortunate position. Beginning in May last, hostile armies have alternately, as the fortune of war vibrated in the scale, traversed every part of our State, carrying ruin and devastation in their train wherever they went, until vast regions, formerly teeming with wealth and productive industry, were laid waste, and to a great extent depopulated. A large part of the pecuniary losses resulting from the ruin of the people in those districts falls to the lot of the business community in this city, who are constantly in the relation of creditors towards the back country; and while the people of St. Louis suffered their full share of the immediate burdens and losses of the war, they are still further impoverished by the ruin of their debtors.

But worse remains to be told. In July, 1861, all transportation and communication by the Mississippi to the south of us was stopped by order the the Government of the United States as a belligerent measure, and we were thus cut off entirely and suddenly from the most important and valuable part of our trade-- the export of the agricultural produce of the Upper Mississippi valley to our best customers: the Southern States, Mexico, the West Indies, &c. The magnitude of this trade . . .

The mayor then mentioned the four consecutive years of crop failures that effected area farmers, including Ulysses S. Grant in South County, before discussing the city's role as the market for the Mississippi River Valley.

Our city had become the great market of the Mississippi valley for groceries and manufactures, possessing facilities for the transaction of a trade as enormous as that of any city on the continent. This great traffic is for the present totally cut off, and it is as yet utterly

impossible to foresee when it will be reopened. That our manufacturing industry has suffered, from the causes above enumerated
. . . still the fact of utter stagnation in most branches of manufacture is plainly evident to every observer . . . , our population is
impoverished, and our industry for a length of time doomed to a
forced idleness, it must be evident to every reflecting man that the
financial concerns of our local government must be very greatly
affected by the very general distress. Soon after entering upon the
discharge of the duties of this office, in April, 1861, I found that
the very heavy reduction in our revenues caused by the decrease
in the value of property, and the complete stagnation of all kinds
of business, would make it impossible for us to meet all demands
upon our teasury for the current year.

The mayor sought to ease anxiety of creditors with the following
statement.

What we now owe, and for the present are unble to pay, shall be
paid as soon as we can earn enough to do so. The often tested and
well known elasticity and recuperative power of our people is so
great, that, aided by the natural advantages of our position (which
cannot be taken away from us), it is safe to predict that our present
helplessness will not be of long duration.

Circular, March 20, 1862, "To the Creditors of the City of St. Louis,"
Mayor's Messages, 4-6, St. Louis Public Library.

John How, John Riggin, and W. Patrick

Police Commissioners

Political forces turned the St. Louis Police Department upside down during the first year of the war. Recognizing that control of the city's police could shape the fate of St. Louis, Confederate sympathizing Governor Claiborne Fox Jackson had established a police board in the spring of 1861. The governor appointed the board members to maintain Confederate power within the city.

After Governor Jackson fled Jefferson City, and Hamilton Gamble became the provisional governor, the original board president "resigned, and his associates were removed by Governor Gamble, who appointed the undersigned, the present Commissioners, in their stead."

In the first annual report, the new commissioners document a Confederate absconding with police funds and young waitresses turning to prostitution.

These excerpts from the report also discuss changes in manpower, the refusal of the previous, secessionist board to account for its expenditures, and the loyalty of the current officers to the Union.

The first Board [the secessionists] assuming to consider it within the line of their duty to watch the acts of the United States troops, increased the police force at one time to 320 men, including officers. When the present Board came into office, it had been reduced to 207. The police now consists of 175 men, including officers.

The report referred to the money spent while the secessionists were in office, before addressing the current circumstances.

The present Board have been embarrassed by the illegal and inexcusable detention by the first Board of all the vouchers for money paid, and all the books, excepting the record of proceedings hereinbefore referred to. They refused our official demand for them, denying our authority to supersede them.

The late Treasurer of the Board is supposed to have absconded, and taken refuge among the traitors to his country, with several thousand dollars of the police fund, for which we have caused a suit to be instituted against the sureties on his official bond.

The Commissioners would respectfully recommend that the honorable City Council should so amend the ordinances regulating licenses of beer saloons, and places of exhibition, where young girls are employed to carry refreshments to visitors, as to lessen an increasing evil, and the demoralizing tendency of employing young girls in that capacity; many of them by their dress and conduct, appear to be prostitutes or in the way of becoming such.

The commissioners recommended the same appropriations for police as the 1860 budget provided, before stating that they had purged the department of secessionists.

We have purged the police of many, for their loud and frequent expression of secession sentiments, and their sympathy with traitors and rebels, and for inefficiency, &c., until there remains very few on the rolls that may not be considered policemen of the first class.

And we flatter ourselves that at no time heretofore were the police of the city more active and efficient than they are at this time.

We acknowledge our indebtedness to our Chief of Police, John E.D. Couzens, whose great practical experience has contributed so much to the discipline and efficiency of the force.

All which is respectfully submitted.

John How,

John Riggin,

W. Patrick,

Police Commissioners of the City of St. Louis

Police Commissioners' Report, April 29, 1862, Mayor's Messages, St. Louis Public Library.

BERNARD G. FARRAR

The provost-marshal-general of the Department of the Mississippi, Bernard G. Farrar, issued a special order (Special Orders No. 300) on June 17, requiring all persons in St. Louis suspected of disloyal sympathies to take the oath of allegiance to the United States government. All persons "well known by their conduct, bearing, converstion, or companions to be disloyal shall be required to give bond for the observance of their oath." Nearly a thousand Southern sympathizers in St. Louis received a circular calling upon them to take the following oath.

I, _____ _____, county of ____, State of ____, do solemnly swear that I will support, protect, and defend the Constitution and government of the United States, and the provisional government of the State of Missouri, against all enemies, whether domestic or foreign; that I will bear true faith, allegiance, and loyalty to the same, any ordinance, resolution, or law of any State Convention or Legislature to the contrary notwithstanding; and, further, that I will well and faithfully perform all the duties which may be required of me by the laws of the United States. And I take this oath without any mental reservation or evasion whatsoever, with a full and clear understanding that death or other punishment by the judgment of a military commission will be the penalty for the violation of this my solemn oath. And I also swear that under no consideration will I go beyond the military lines of the United States forces, so help me God.

Thomas Scharf, History of Saint Louis City and County *(Philadelphia: Louis H. Everts & Co., 1883), 431.*

THE LOUIS PICOT FAMILY

L ouis Picot was an attorney living in Carondelet, then a separate municipality facing the Mississippi River south of St. Louis. He had built a castle-like stone house on a hilltop at 6500 Minnesota Avenue (next to the Sisters of St. Joseph convent), that was a landmark to the passing rivermen. The prosperous attorney had publicly defended the Union, but he was quickly seen as a traitor when he flew a Rebel flag. He fled rather than take a loyalty oath to the Union.

Though this account of "A Civil War Incident" is in third person, it appears to have been told or written by one of Picot's children, who would have witnessed the event. The account refers to businessman and civic leader Henry T. Blow, a neighbor who supported abolition and Union. Blow's history was tied to that of Dred Scott, whose failed legal journey to win his freedom from slavery moved the nation closer to Civil War. Though Blow's father had owned Scott decades earlier, Henry T. Blow testified on Scott's behalf and the Blow family financially supported Scott's legal suit and subsequently freed him.

A CIVIL WAR INCIDENT

During the Civil War, this was a marked spot. Mr. Picot was a Virginian and was opposed to secession. At the invitation of Mr. Henry T. Blow, he made numerous Union speeches. But like General Robert E. Lee, when Virginia went out of the Union, Mr. Picot cast his fortunes with his state. Shortly afterwards he was called on to take the . . . oath, but fled to Canada to avoid it.

Reports went out that he was stirring sedition in the South and confiscation of his property and persecution of his family were inaugurated. A hotel that Mr. Picot was building on Broadway near Biddle, afterward known as the Girard House, and which was latterly acquired by Dr. J.H. McLean, was the first to be seized. Two months afterwards Ex-Governor Fletcher, then a Colonel of Missouri Volunteers and Commandant at Carondelet, went to the Picot home at four o'clock one afternoon and presented an order to Mrs. Picot to take her family, abandon the house and leave the state. Two hours, the order said, would be allowed and were she not gone, the whole family would be sent to prison. The little matron was plucky and without a murmur, began prepartions to leave her home of luxury with her six young children, as a penniless outcast. Just then, however, Henry T. Blow rode hastily up, entered the parlor and after greeting the Colonel, said: "This order is an outrage, Sir, or is evidently an error."

"But a soldier knows no errors, and must obey," said Colonel Fletcher. "It is a painful order for me to execute, but my duty is inexorable."

"In this case the order will not be executed at least for two weeks. I will stand between you, Sir, and the government, and pledge you immunity," was the reply, and it was compromised on that basis. Two weeks after that, the order was rescinded, and even the banished head of the family was allowed to return. So faithful was Mr. Blow to his old friend that he would not even allow the Federals to station a guard about the home to, as he said, "Insult the ladies by the presence of soldiers."

"A Civil War Incident," Picot Family Papers, Missouri History Museum Archives.

LOUIS PHILIP FUSZ

The character of life in St. Louis had altered after a year of war. Members of the old French and Southern communities lamented the passing of the old ways.

French native, and Southern sympathizer Louis Fusz kept a journal throughout the war. On Sunday August 31, 1862, the young Frenchman described the funeral of Mrs. P. Chouteau Jr. held at the Cathedral. He wrote that her pall bearers were her "old slaves." In this passage, Fusz wrote as if he was witnessing more than an individual's passing, but the death of a way of life and of a social structure. He used an antiquated term, "relict," to describe her. Though the term often refers to a widow, he was likely indicating that she was from a by-gone era.

Sunday August 31st 1862

On last Sunday there died here an old relict of St. Louis. Mrs. P. Chouteau, Jr. departed her life at 3 o'clock in the afternoon of that day at the age of near 69.

. . . Poor old lady, kind, affectionate, and familiar, her manners bridged the distance separating wealth from poverty and her affability made the latter forget of any difference. For sometime on her death bed she received the consulations of the church and at last she slept away, surrounded by her husband, her children and grandchildren. Thus one more link of the past is broken and they who only yesterday were present now live but in history, in the remembrance of friends and connections.

On Tuesday morning the funeral took place; her old slaves were the coffin bearers; when with slow and measured steps, their swarthy faces came into view at the entrance of the old Cathedral, a thrill of emotion overpowered me and the tears came streaming through my eyes; vainly I struggled but unavailingly and I had to let nature have her course with me. The scene was so impressive, the funeral toll, always thrilling to me, now had a double effect. In these days of discord, old customs passing away, I felt that in a short time a harsh, unfeeling, egotistical world would have full sway over places rendered dear by sweet recollections. She was buried in her lot at the Calvary Cemetery and by her side is the vacant place awaiting in its turn the remains of her husband, P. Chouteau, Jr.

Louis Philip Fusz Diary, Vol. I, 24-25, Missouri History Museum Archives.

THE FASHIONABLE SECESH
OF ST. LOUIS

ARebel mail bag carrying "secesh" letters was captured in early
September of 1862. The *Daily Missouri Democrat* published the
letters on September 10. The *Globe* described the letters as offering "Rare Revelations" and an "Inside View of the Fashionable Secesh of St.
Louis." It was considered, "The richest expose of the season . . ."

In many cases codes instead of the full names were given in the letters, which undoubtedly added to the speculation and gossip once the
letters were published.

The letters include many mentions of civilians traveling both in the
North and South, often to avoid loyalty oaths, military drafts, or even
imprisonment.

Even in response to inconveniences during war, when others were
suffering terribly, the writers possess a sense of privilege and outrage.
Their petulance is particularly harsh in reference to "servants" or slaves,
whose plights had always been tragic and desperate.

Though references to names and events are often vague and confusing, the letters reveal the attitudes of secessionists in St. Louis. The
excerpts that follow—many paragraphs concerning personal matters
were omitted—begin with the first letter published that was addressed
"Dear Sam." It was dated St. Louis, August 23, 1862, and signed, "Your loving sister, Lizzie." After a few personal comments, Lizzie mentioned that
Provisional Missouri Governor Hamilton Gamble had ordered the National
Guard to reorganize.

All the stores are closed at 4 p.m., in order for the militia to drill. S. Laflin, Joe Cabot, and Hatch are on Gray's staff. A week or two ago officers were appointed to go to every house and enroll all the names of men over eighteen and under forty-five. They say they are going to commence drafting next week. The last two days they have been impressing men by going to different drinking shops and theaters, and even the jail, and taking men from them and obliging them to enlist. Gamble, in a speech made a few nights ago, advocated shooting the "guerrillas," the "non-combatant secesh" to be assessed and then sent South. Picot's property has all been confiscated; his family ordered to leave their house and everything in it. They lived in Carondelet.

In the next paragraph, Lizzie writes of another local girl as if she is a collaborator.

I have heard a great many say they do not think L____e G_____s deserving all the praise given her; at any rate she is full as kind to the Federals. She is walking, riding and flirting with them all the time. I can assure you there are not many Southern women in St. Louis would speak to a Federal. Her mother has done a great deal, and so have a great many others in a quiet way.

Last winter L____e G_____s and some other young ladies, visited families where there were prisoners every day. They would kiss some of the prisoners every morning and quarrel which should have such a one to walk with or for a beau.

The letter writer added more news on "Friday, 29th." She referred to enclosed newspaper clippings and noted, "We are all rejoicing over the news from Virginia tonight." Her tone is almost annoyed as she reports that slaves were being freed, and then she listed the status of secesh friends.

A great many negroes have been freed in the city lately. Mrs. C___'s (Jim Shaler's mother-in-law) has had a great deal of trouble with some of hers. They have been freed, also some of Colonel O'Fallon's, etc.

I saw Mrs. McP____ a few days ago, and told her what you said of her husband. She was looking well and as cheerful as possible. Mrs. W____ is with her friends in Kentucky. Ned Martin has been banished to Massachusetts. His health is very poor. Jim Douglass is in prison at Alton, for saying at one of the National Guard meetings, that he considered himself a prisoner of war. Mr. Nelson holds forth every Sunday—preaches abolition, etc., every week. One of the things brought against father last winter was his not going there to church. Father is first-rate secesh, but does not like to give anything to help the cause along. You know father well enough to understand that. Mrs. P. is in daily fear that the authorities will give her trouble. Mothers sees her most every day. I wish I could write you more news. I never look at the papers for they are not worth reading.

Your loving sister,
Lizzie.

On August 23, 1862, a letter signed "Miss L." was addressed to "Capt. Bredell," whose family lived on Lafayette Avenue facing Lafayette Park. In the letter, Miss L. mentions John Riggin, Bredell's former baseball team member. In the following excerpts, the writer sometimes sounds spoiled, sometimes sarcastic, but always filled with suppressed anger.

St. Louis is very stupid now. We have nothing in the way of amusement, and there is not the visiting there used to be, for we have no beaux to visit; indeed, our streets would be deserted if it were not for shoulder-straps. Your friend, Mr. Fullerton, is fourth sergeant in the Hallack Guard, and went up to Lexington; but succeeded only in burning and sinking some little boats belonging to private individuals, for which the Democrat urges they should have some public demonstration for their personal bravery.

Mr. Allan P. was yesterday expecting to have quarters furnished him at McDowell's College [then used as a prison]. He has had three notices sent him to report for active duty, but not feeling that way inclined, he paid no attention to them, and was expecting the consequences.

Mr. Pittman has gone to Kentucky to get married. I do not know what we are going to do without him. There were a number of gentlemen left here about the time they thought of drafting, but they are gradually coming back. Mr. Bryan returned yesterday. I suppose the attraction at Glencoe was too strong to allow him to venture far.

Mary L. and I were out last week a few days with Mrs. C. Mrs. Sue B. came over to see us, looking as pretty as ever. Mr. McDowell, I hear, is still devoted. Mary and I had a grand time. We had all the beaux St. Louis could muster, out with us. . . . Miss Fannie B. has been for some time this summer in Kentucky, but is now at home. I expect you have seen her brother, as he left for the South. . . .

After more personal notes, "Miss L." talks about slaves being freed as if her world is topsy-turvy.

Uncle Jeff, is at Niagara, and in yesterday's paper I saw that Berney Farrar had set three of his servants free. It only requires a word from a negro to have any gentleman arrested and imprisoned, so you see what we are coming to.

Our neighbor across the street is as savage as ever. His daughter is Secretary to the "Ladies' Union Aid Society," and her favorite song is "John Brown's bones lie mouldering in the grave," which we have the full benefit of. How some people fall to their proper level!

To your inquiry about the bricklayer, I have heard he is devoted to Miss B., and is very rabid and believes in crushing out the rebellion. I don't speak from personal knowledge of his views, as I have not even a speaking acquaintance with his majesty, who parades the streets in a Federal uniform, and his friend, Mr. L., has been dropped completely by the circle in which he once moved. . . .

The following excerpts reflect a confidence in the Confederate cause, and a growing resentment of the Unionists and abolitionists.

We went out on the afternoon train, and danced all night, and came home in the morning. Ze Chambers has gone to Ireland to visit his relatives. He left very suddenly, as a great many others did. Eugene Pendleton is up in Burlington, Missouri, having run off from the supposed drafting; and Mr. Haynes has gone to Canada. I think it contemptible in young men who object to fight in the Northern army going off to such places, when they might go South; but perhaps they would not be much of an addition to the army . . .

John Riggin is in town again, and I expect there is soon to be a fight, as he always leaves about that time. He was up here before and brought a negro man that he had stolen from the South.

. . . We have waited a long time, but I trust that before many months you will all come to release us from the hateful fetters that bind us, for nearly every day, they come out with some new order; and this morning a man signing himself "Justice" thinks the women and children should be sent with all the traitors out of the Federal lines . . .

Poor Mrs. Doctor C. is having a hard lot, they have banished her from Missouri and freed all her servants.

Miss L.S. spent last winter in Washington where she caught a beau—Lieut. Foster—and is to be married soon. She heard he was killed in the battle before Richmond and bought her mourning, but he is still alive (I am sorry to say as long as he is a Federal.) Miss S. was in town for a day or two this week. She is very well and Mr. Tennent is devoted to her; but I think she has concluded to wait until some one of you handsome staff officers come, and I hope you and your friend, Mr. Holland, will soon give us an opportunity of having a big party, as one of your friends has promised on your arrival in St. Louis. Remember me kindly to Generals Phifer and Armstrong. I heard the latter was married, and mean enough to write it to Mag last Sunday.

The letter closed with,

Remember me to all my friends South, and if that brother of mine is with you, tell him to send me word. I had a letter from him from Springfield, in which he said he was going back to Mississippi.

I have set you such a good example that I hope to hear again from you, and with my best wishes and kindest regards for yourself,

Believe me your friend,
Miss L.

"Rare Revelations. Inside View of the Fashionable Secesh of St. Louis," Daily Missouri Democrat, *September 10, 1862, Chouteau Family Papers 1861-65, Missouri History Museum Archives.*

James M. Carpenter

In several letters, St. Louisan James M. Carpenter described wartime circumstances in St. Louis to associates who were out of town. The Kentucky native was the bookkeeper and cashier for the executors of the estate of Judge Bryan Mullanphy. When the Mullanphy Relief Board was organized, he was elected its first secretary. While in that role, he studied law and then became interested in real estate. The excerpts below tell of wartime inflation, of assessments on Southern sympathizing friends, and warn of the pervasiveness of the military draft. The letters reflect a surprising mobility among St. Louisans during the war.

In his letter to "Jno O T Delany, Esq" of October 6, 1862, he wrote:

Unless you have some physical debility on account of which you could get an Exemption Certificate from Military duty you had <u>best not return here</u> as you would be compelled to enroll and join a Regiment for State service or go to Prison. Squads of Provost guards are continually [patrolling] the streets forcing <u>every man</u> they meet to show his Certificate of Enrollment or Exemption. Enquiries have been made of me as to your whereabouts which I of course satisfied. John Waddell and a great many others have gone to the Southern Army from this County.

John Murphy has been on active duty with the Enrolled Militia guarding the Bridges and track of the Iron Mountain RR and all the State Militia will be ordered so soon as the Rebels come up from Arkansas which they are doing about 40,000 strong. Gen Schofield has gone down to Springfield to thrash them. There has been a very bloody engagement at Corinth between Price & Grant & Rosecranz in which the papers say Price was defeated.

Abolition & Confiscation is the order of the day now.

Your Mother is at the Fifth Avenue Hotel NY I shall be glad to hear from you.

Very Truly Yours,
Jas M Carpenter

In a letter to "Jno O T Delany, Esq. New York" and dated St. Louis, November 12, 1862, Carpenter discussed the wartime economy's effect on the price of coal.

Everything is advancing very rapidly in price owing to the great depreciation in "Green Backs" which are worth about .66 c on the dollar, for instance wood is $10.00 per cord—coal .20c per bushel. Potatoes this time last year were worth .15c per bushel are selling now at 1.00 per bushel &c &c. Dry goods have more than doubled in price. So also everything we consume, and where the end of all this is God only can tell. Rents in Central localities for dwellings have advanced say twenty per cent on Olive Pine Locust & such streets. Business of every Kind out of the Army line is extremely dull, and the heavy Government Tax comes hard on our already greatly overtaxed people.

In his letter to Mrs. Octavia Boyce in New York, on November 27, 1862, Carpenter recounted the assessments that Confederate sympathizers had to pay.

Dear Madam

There is nothing of much consequence going on here except the assessment of Southern friends & sympathiezers—Mrs Graham was assessed Twelve Hundred dollars, Mrs. Frost Twenty two hundred & ___nty five dollars besides having all her rents stopped, Thos B. Hudson I hear Six hundred. D.A. January Fifteen hundred dollars

R.A. Bau__s Twenty Two hundred dollars. Lar____e Bissell & many others one Thousand each—I learn that about eight hundrd notices have been served and the Committee of Requisition are still at work So you may know that very few escape. Unless they are very loyal like you and myself who of course will not be assessed because we have always been opposed to Secession and hope to see it one united Country, living happily and prosperously under that good old Constitution our Fathers fought & died for.

Mullanphy Family Papers, 1861-65, Missouri History Museum Archives.

ABSALOM C. GRIMES

The military had transformed the McDowell Medical College into a prison housing captured Confederate soldiers, Confederates charged as "bush-whackers," spies or mail carriers, and also deserters and delinquents from the Union side. The incarcerated included farmers, riverboat pilots, and many prominent citizens of Missouri.

The odd-looking medical school had a fortress-like appearance. Dr. Joseph Nash McDowell built the gray stone structure in 1847 on the northwest corner of Eighth and Gratiot streets. (The site is just south of Busch Stadium.) It consisted of a large octagonal building of gray stone, topped by a domed cupola. Two wings with arched or square windows flanked the octagon.

Outspoken in his Confederate sympathies, Dr. McDowell left St. Louis to join Confederate forces in 1861. At first, Union forces used the castle-like building as a barracks. It was converted into a prison, accepting its first prisoners on December 24, 1861.

Among the more well-known prisoners was riverboat pilot Absalom C. Grimes, a famous mail carrier and spy, who recounted his escape from the Gratiot Street Prison.

Gratiot Street Prison

I was then sent to the Gratiot Street prison, Sept. 2, 1862, the date being inscribed on the wall, and brought for trial, on the charge of being a rebel mail-carrier and spy, before a military commission of which Gen. John B. Gray was the president. They brought me in guilty, and I was sentenced to death, the day of execution being fixed for the second Friday in October, 1862. I was placed in solitary confinement, with handcuffs, ball and chain. The room was about fourteen feet square, in the interior of the building, and was formerly used by Dr. McDowell as a back-parlor. There was a window on one side, and on the other side there were folding-doors in the partition separating it from the front parlor on the Eighth Street side, which was used as a female prison. The folding-doors between were securely nailed up. In the female prison were then confined two well-known ladies and two other ladies. One day the ladies handed me a bottle of chloroform, and asked me if I wanted it. I answered it in the affirmative. I took it through the jointure of the folding-doors, which could be pressed apart near the bottom for the purpose." [His attempts to use the chloroform on guards failed, so he developed a new escape plan.]

In prosecuting my plan for escape, I during the day would lay on my mattress in one corner of the room and cut a narrow groove across three of the floor planks. This I did in two places, and split the tongues of the grooves with a dirk-knife given to me by the women through a rat-hole in the folding-doors. After I got the planks up in the floor I could replace them, and by inserting thin strips of wood in the cut places, the floor looked perfectly sound and was not observed by the prison officials. I used to open the hole at night, and by crawling along under the floor, which was from two to four feet from the ground, in a northeast direction, brought me immediately under the room where the ladies were in, and with a bar of iron and a large butcher-knife, which had been passed to me by a brother-prisoner named Chapman, I commenced making a breach through a wall which would let me into an alley-way. The implements were procured by Chapman from the cook-room. While I was working at the wall, the women, in accordance with a previous understanding, would dance and move the chairs about, and thereby keep up a racket so as to drown any noise I would be making in burrowing a hole through the wall. At the same time one of the women would watch the door and window in my room through a crack in the folding-doors between their room and mine, and with a string attached to the old rocking-chair, she would rock the chair once in a while, which led the guard to believe that I was lying on the mattress and rocking the chair with my foot, the chair being placed directly between the mattress and the window, with a coat thrown over the back of it. The guards could not get into my room without first going to the office and getting Officer Bishop, or his clerk, Streeter, to unlock the door. It took me two nights to cut through the wall, which was of brick eighteen inches thick, and the foundation of stone two feet thick.

After effecting a breach through the wall, I knew that it would bring me into a narrow alley between the old stone building and McDowell's residence, which was about four feet wide, and filled with cord-wood. Knowing that the wood-pile was there before, I told Chapman to climb over the far end of the wood-pile before roll-call in his room, on the night agreed upon for our escape, and secrete himself, and then to pile the wood back, so I would have no wood-pile to contend with when I came to the alley.

Our plan being thus nearly completed, the night of the 2d of October, a few days previous to the time fixed for my execution, was set to carry it into effect.

My plan not being disarranged by any untoward event, I started in the dead of night to carry out the enterprise. I passed down through the hole in the floor underneath the women's prison-room to the breach in the wall, where I disengaged myself from my shackles and a thirty-two-pound shell, but found that Chapman, who was by prearrangement to meet me, had piled back of him all the cord-wood he possibly could get back, yet I had to pull nearly half a cord in through the breach in the wall, which I piled up behind me under the floor. I then gained the alley-way, which brought me and Chapman together. We found on the outside of the alley a two-inch poplar partition, which shut off our entrance to the street. I then commenced to cut through the plank partition with a dirk-knife, only having to cut a groove cross one sixteen-inch plank two inches thick. It took just twenty minutes to do the job. After the hole was cut, Chapman looked at his watch, and it was just twenty minutes of twelve, midnight. As we had the guard to pass, we waited until twelve o'clock, when the guards would be relieved.

Scharf, 420.

1863

". . . we must either conquer or die"
—Edward Bates at the Carondelet Union Iron Works, July 4, 1863

On January 1, 1863, the Emancipation Proclamation enobled the Civil War. The year 1863 brought decisive but horrific battles in both the East, where great armies stumbled into a massive three-day battle at Gettysburg, and in the West, where Vicksburg surrendered after a long and deadly siege. The exhaustion from the endless death of the battlefields erupted in a new kind of violence, deadly draft riots in New York.

In St. Louis, the year 1863 brought more refugees, more wounded, more prisoners, and a deadly riot. On January 1, however, the *Daily Missouri Republican* indicated that there was some reason for optimism. Under the headline "Local News" St. Louisans read the editorial statement, "Such a war as ours must soon reach its natural termination. So vast a war, involving expenditures in a scale of enormity surpassing all precedent, must neccessarily be short-lived. But passing events indicate the same probability. No man who ever loved the American Union can but hope that it will terminate in re-etablishing the old cordial relations between its several States. With such good fortune in immediate view we can the more cheerfully wish all whome we address a Happy New Year, in the warm trust that the return of peace and the restoration of the Union, will make the present year to all a happier one than the past."

On January 3, St. Louisans read the President's Proclamation on page one of the *Daily Missouri Republican*. It stated, "That on the first day of January, in the year of our Lord 1863, all persons held as slaves within any State, or designate parts of a State, the people, where of shall then be in rebellion against the United States, shall be then, thenceforth and forever free." The proclamation did not free the slaves in Missouri because the state was technically not in rebellion against the United States. The proclamation did guarantee that the military would recognize and maintain the freedom of liberated slaves from the Confederacy.

With the proclamation, the war was transformed. Many liberated slaves made their way to St. Louis. The proclamation also declared "that such persons of suitable condition, will be received into the armed service of the United States." Soon St. Louisans would be seeing African-Americans wearing the Union blue.

The St. Louis arsenal, iron works, and boatyards were continually busy supplying the war effort in the West. And much of that effort was focused on Vicksburg, which was the Confederate citadel on the Mississippi River. Facing the river, built into hills, and protected by swamps it seemed unconquerable. But as long as it stood in Confederate hands, the Union was thwarted. Grant understood that, and kept tightening the noose around Vicksburg in a campaign that required months.

Perhaps because St. Louisans filled Grant's Union ranks while other St. Louisans defended the Confederate stronghold, the people of St. Louis realized the strategic importance of Vicksburg. The summer of 1863, citizens, from the shopkeepers to Julia Dent Grant, waited anxiously for news from the Vicksburg campaign. Meanwhile, great armies in the East stumbled into an enormous battle at Gettysburg.

While rumors and news were slowly creeping in from these great battlefields, word spread quickly across St. Louis about an Independence Day celebration in North City. Too many unruly soldiers and too much liquor and beer turned a holiday festivity in a public park into deadly mayhem.

While civic leaders and citizens investigated the riot in Hyde Park and debated allowing beer concessions in public parks, charities reorganized and expanded to serve more refugees and the many wounded from Vicksburg. The Freedmen's Relief Association emerged from the Sanitary Commission to assist the slaves freed by the Emancipation Proclamation.

One visitor to St. Louis in 1863, the architect of New York's Central Park Frederick Law Olmsted, felt that St. Louis had suffered from the war more than any other city outside the Confederacy.

FREDERICK LAW OLMSTED

During the spring of 1863, Frederick Law Olmsted, the founder of American landscape architecture and the nation's foremost park maker, visited St. Louis. Though Olmsted had already served as superintendent and architect-in-chief of construction for New York's Central Park, at the beginning of the Civil War he was the administrative head of the U.S. Sanitary Commission.

While in St. Louis, Olmsted reviewed the hospitals and Benton Barracks. Though his own career was only beginning, his comments on St. Louis reflected his ability to analyze a whole community, its texture, commerce, civic ornaments, and weaknesses. In his journal entries, he noted the streetscapes of St. Louis, its Southern flavor, its strong middle-class population, and related a conversation with a former mayor. He described a dinner with a prominent St. Louisan of Southern heritage, likely James Yeatman who served as president of the Western Sanitary Commission. He visited with Henry Shaw and noted his disappointment at seeing Missouri Botanical Garden, then only in its infancy and only a seed of what it would soon become. He wrote with hope about Shaw's ideas for creating what would become Tower Grove Park.

St. Louis.
[April 4-11, 1863]

In the general street aspect of St. Louis there is nothing peculiar-
ly Western. It is substantially built—more so than most Eastern
towns—more so than New York on an average. There are few
buildings of notable character, many which are respectable. The
same is true of the town socially, I judge. We dined one day at a
small villa. The people—well-bred and neither genteel nor styl-
ish—were chiefly of Southern birth and of modified Southern
manners. I should probably have said Western, if I had not become familiar with those which are Southern. The wines were
nearly the same as at a Charleston dinner of similar scale, the talk
about them was a playfully held but natural remnant of the serious
Charleston habit of wine-talk. There were some good paintings
and an exquisite small statue by an Italian sculptor; the grounds
had a plantation rudeness, inequality of keeping and untidiness.
The family, hot and strong Unionists, hating the rebels and zealous
with newly emancipated repugnance to Slavery, had nevertheless
an obvious, though unconfessed and probably unconscious pride
in being Southern. But this they would, if it had been demonstrated to them, have themselves regarded as a weakness, possibly;
what they never thought of concealing or suppressing or restrain-
ing from its utmost outpouring was their satisfaction in being St.
Louisians. No subject was talked of that did not give occasion for
some new method, (always used confidently and with certainty that
it was kindness to do so) for trumpeting St. Louis. It was the same
with every man & woman we met in St. Louis. The devout dwell-
ers in Mecca do not worship the holy city more than every child
of St. Louis, his city. It happened that I was enough interested to
enjoy this. It was what I wanted. And the most notable thing I
learned of St. Louis was the pleasure of the people to talk about
it—what it had been, what it would be.

The two things which interested me most, after the poorly

contrived barracks of immense extent, and the military hospitals, were the Mercantile Library and the botanic gardens of Mr.____ promised by him to be given at his death to the city. The Botanic Garden greatly disappointed me—simply because I had sometime before read an account of it in the Western advertising style in which it was magnified by adjective force, many hundredfold.

Henry Shaw was in the beginning stages of developing his Missouri Botanical Garden, which would eventually grow to meet Olmsted's expectations. Olmsted wrote that the tremendous demand for and use of the Fair Grounds, established in 1856 on North Grand, demonstrated St. Louisans desire for an expansive public park.

And this in a town west of the Mississippi, nearly one third of the population of which have been brought across the Atlantic from Germany, as steerage-passengers, and every man in which, of the rich as well as the poor, seems enslaved to a habit of incessant activity and labor to enlarge the supply, at St. Louis, of the material wants of men. The tide of commerce incessantly flows through every man's brain. You perceive it as strongly in those of the quieter callings—the teachers, preachers, physicians, as in others. All are busy with the foundation-laying of civilization. Some stones for the superstructure are being set but they are so let in to the foundations that the sense of commercial speculation is never wholly lost.

Out of domestic life, the Mercantile Library was the most respectable matter that I came in contact with in St. Louis. A very large hall with a goodly number of men and women, boys and girls, reading books, and looking at statues and paintings. These were not all very good, but enough to feed that part of a man's nature through which works of art do him good, better than one man in a million is fed by unassociated reachings out for such aliment. Even the Mercantile Library, however, is mercantile and, as I inferred from some account of its rent transactions, would hardly exist—certainly would not be what it is—had not the plan for it possessed a certain element of good trading. I think it was, in some way or other, apropos of the Mercantile Library that a gentleman said to me: "People here like very much to associate all their benevolence with business. Almost any benevolent enterprise will be taken hold of liberally here, if you can show that it carries a business advantage to our city with it. We are all very fond of feeling that we are driving business and philanthropy harnessed together in the same team." An enormous building designed for a hotel but not occupied, was pointed out to us.

"Why is it not occupied?"

"It really is not needed as a hotel. It would not pay expenses, I suppose, if it were opened, now."

"Why was it built then?"

"The capital was supplied for it by the property owners in this part of the city because they thought it would have a favorable influence upon the value of property. They have in effect, for this reason, given a bonus of several hundred thousand dollars in order to get the finest hotel in the city established where it will help to bring their lots and buildings more into public view. That is a kind of advertising which is very much resorted to here. Our churches are built, in that way, a great deal."

I was glad to notice that the public schools were an object of pride with the citizens. The buildings are large. I did not enter them nor meet any of the teachers.

In passing through a part of the town occupied almost exclusively by Germans, on a warm Sunday when the windows were generally open, I noticed much new and smart furniture and that the women were nearly all smartly dressed. I saw no squalid poverty except among negroes & fugitives from the seat of war, I did not see a beggar in St. Louis. I do not recollect that I saw a policeman, though I did more than once see and experience the need of one. It is certainly from no action of the law or good regulations or public provision for paupers that no beggar & so little poverty is seen. Yet St. Louis, it is generally supposed, suffers much more than any other considerable town out of the rebel states from the war. Its growth had been recently very rapid until it was arrested by the war. I asked an old resident, distinguished for his interest in the poor & needy, and who had been a mayor of the city, "How generally have poor, laboring men and families been found, in your observation, to improve their condition, after they have moved to St. Louis?"

He answered, "invariably," meaning, no doubt, that any exceptions were of plainly accidental character.

"Can you see that the children of those who came here longest ago are now generally fit for higher social duties and of a higher rank as men than their fathers?"

"Universally so; with the Germans especially; they become Americans, with all the American characteristics."

There are probably a larger number of men of what would be considered moderate wealth in the middle class of England, in St. Louis, than in any town of its size in Europe. I asked my friend, the ex-mayor, "How many of these came to St. Louis comparatively poor men?"

"There is scarcely one that did not begin here by sweeping out his employer's store or office, and that is true of most of our very wealthiest men also—our bankers and capitalists. We nearly all began here with nothing but our heads and hands."

This being the case it is really more marvelous how well the people live within their own houses than how very poorly they live out of their own houses.

The Papers of Frederick Law Olmsted, Volume IV. Jane Turner Censer, editor, Defending the Union: The Civil War and the U.S. Sanitary Commission, 1861-1863 *(Baltimore: The Johns Hopkins University Press, 1986), 585-88.*

EMILY ELIZABETH PARSONS

When the Civil War broke out, Emily Elizabeth Parsons of Massachusetts was a woman with a mission—to serve the wounded. Her disabilities, blinded in one eye, lamed in one ankle, and left partially deaf by scarlet fever, could not stop her. Her father, a professor of law at Harvard, stated that she had all the "opportunities which offer themselves to unmarried women who seek for them, until in 1861 the war of the Rebellion broke out." It was with reluctance that he accepted her determination to become a nurse. At the age of thirty-seven, Parsons enrolled in nursing school at Massachusetts General Hospital. Throughout her service, Parsons was aflicted with regular bouts of illness. The illnesses and exhausting character of the work, however, could not keep Parsons from returning to her mission.

Following her training, she was placed in charge of a ward attending fifty wounded soldiers at Fort Schuyler Military Hospital on Long Island. "In a few weeks she was summoned, somewhat urgently, to St. Louis." She took charge of the nursing department on board one of the river steamers that picked up the sick and wounded in Vicksburg. With the Western Sanitary Commission in St. Louis, she was made supervisor of nurses at the hospital at Benton Barracks.

After her death, her father published her correspondence detailing her experiences as a war nurse, *Memoir of Emily Elizabeth Parsons*. The memoir reflects the new efforts, begun in the Crimean War, to care for the battlefield wounded.

These excerpts from her letters

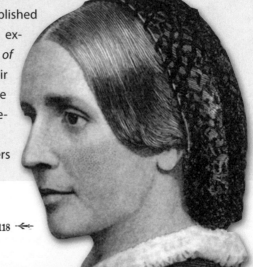

written in St. Louis during 1863 recall the challenges of keeping the wounded comfortable in a subtropical summer, the news of and importance of the surrender of Vicksburg, and the saga of one nurse whose husband died at Gettysburg.

July 7.—I have finished my morning rounds, and have a few minutes: do you want them? I should like a good New England eastwind; it would be perfectly refreshing, the air is so sultry to-day. I do not think the heat here so hard to bear as it is with you; it is not such a dry heat, not so burning, but neither is it so healthy. I get along very well, and drink as much water as I want. I suppose I have got through my acclimatizing process; I hope I have. The men seem mending: we are ready for more.

Afternoon.—There is immense excitement,—news that Vicksburg is taken! One of the principal streets of St. Louis is lined with flags. We shall have sick and wounded enough now.

Benton Barracks Hospital,
July 8.

Dear Mother, — . . . The news about Vicksburg is confirmed, and all are duly excited; being on the same river brings it very near to us. The river is now open,—but I tremble to think at what a probable cost. It is extremely hot here, and must be still hotter there. *Thousands* of men are wounded and sick: I hope we shall have them here. Our men are convalescing fast; that is, the greater part. We have over a thousand, sending off as fast as we can to convalescent camps and hospitals, to make room for the newcomers: we shall be very full. This is what we have been waiting for; till Vicksburg fell, they could only send a limited number of the sick; now all will be sent that can possibly be moved, either here or to Memphis. It is not so healthy there as here; therefore as many will be sent north as can be; they travel on the boats in beds quite well. I wish it were not so intensely hot; it is hard for the sick,—this month and August will be like a fiery furnace. I am glad I am here, able to do something. As I told one of my nurses this morning, it is of no use minding the heat; we must make up our minds in the beginning to bear it this month. August and September are very hot; but in September we have some cool days, and the nights are then cooler than the days, which is a great comfort after working all day. Winter will come before we know it. I am drinking new milk for supper now; that has done me good; I buy it at the *sutler's*; she keeps a cow. I have what the calf does not want; I am afraid he does not love me. . . . Is not the news all around good? Lee in retreat, or cut off, which is still better, and here, this long and trying siege over. These were the two points on which so much has depended lately. I do not think you realize the immense importance of the opening of the Mississippi. It alters the position of the whole army of the West, and gives the greatest blow to the rebels. It was their stronghold; and they clung to it with full a knowledge of the fact. The Rebel general, Garnett, was the husband of one of my nurses; she saw his death in the papers this morning; she told me of it. He ran away from her with some one else, disposed of his property so that she could not get any of it,—they were wealthy,—then entered the rebel army. Now he is dead. His wife is a beautiful woman, I should think about twenty-five. She has clung to the hope that he would return to her. She is obliged to do something for her support, I understand. This is a hard world to some. The losses have been very heavy on both sides; many officers gone. My other nurses had relatives at Vicksburg; one other a husband, others brothers and friends. I have to try to help patients and nurses both now. I hope help will be sent to us if we need it. I found in one of the wards a strong man of forty,—his lip quivering so he could hardly speak to me. His son was in the fight, and he has not heard whether he is alive or dead; and so it is, all round.

One of the boys here is very ill; his father came to see him, and found him asleep. When the boy woke there was his father by his bedside. You may imagine the meeting! The old father sits by the bedside fanning him, and he lies with his hand on his father's knee. There is an old man here who has been running down for some time, and so homesick! A few days ago his wife got here; there was a general rejoicing over her in the ward; we were so glad she had come to him. The nurses congratulated them both; it has done him real good. There was another man here very ill, growing worse daily. I wrote to his wife to come to him; and one day when I entered the ward, there she was! I got a warm greeting from her. She brightened him up, nursed him as only a wife can, night and day. I let her stay in the ward, sleeping in the lady nurses' room. He by and by began to mend, and was well enough last week to go home with his wife. If he gets well I do believe it will be due to her; I think she saved his life. Is not that a happy thought for a wife?

In a letter to her mother dated "Benton Barracks Hospital, July 12, 1863, she wrote,

On Thursday many more sick came, mostly wounded. It was a very hot day, and we had our hands full. As I went from ward to ward, I could not help thinking how many there were still unhelped. I found many so exhausted they could not eat. I had a quantity of broth and soup provided, that they could *drink*, and it did them good. If they can be brought up that first stage of exhaustion, it is a great point gained. . . .

Later in the letter, she described the celebration of the fall of Vicksburg.

The city was brilliantly illuminated yesterday, and music and flags to give it all due eclat. I did not go in, for Dr. Russell did not think it best for the lady nurses to go, as there was no one to take care of them, . . . So I staid at home. We had an afternoon celebration out here. Some of the employes subscribed, and procured the services of an excellent band. The Doctor ordered an excellent dinner of various good things, and had a platform erected in the grove, and seats carried out, so that the men could celebrate it in their own fashion. About eleven, the band appeared in an open car decorated with flags, and drawn by four horses. They drove into the gates, preceded by the provost-sergeant on horseback, playing the national airs. In this style they drove slowly round all the hospital buildings, then to the stand. After dinner, we all went down; the ladies had *reserved seats* near the platform. The Doctor was on the platform, but the soldiers had the meeting after their own fashion, and the speaking was very good. You would be surprised to hear how well the soldiers speak. They fear nobody, and speak in the most graphic manner.

Emily Elizabeth Parsons, Memoir of Emily Elizabeth Parsons *(Boston: Little, Brown & Co., 1880), 117-123.*

ANNE EWING LANE

Anger, resentment, bitterness, and vicious racism are sprinkled through the family and neighborhood news in the letters of Anne Ewing Lane to her sister Sarah Lane Glasgow. Anne and Sarah were the daughters of Dr. William Carr Lane, who served as the city's first mayor from 1823 to 1829 and again from 1837 to 1840. The Lanes supported the South. Her father passed away at the beginning of 1863.

Sarah and her husband, William Glasgow Jr., who was a Unionist, were living in Wiesbaden, Germany, during the War.

Letters from Anne in St. Louis to her sister in Germany included war news, affairs in St. Louis, mentions of assessments demanded of secessionists, and accounts that show the hardships the war imposed to their Southern friends.

Anne felt oppressed and spied upon. In the spring of 1862, she complained, "The dutch and the darkies are the only free people here now." The music from the German beer gardens was like salt in her wounds. Her letters reflect a society of Confederates that kept more and more to themselves as the Union's grip on the city strengthened. Though they saw themselves outnumbered, they still dreamed of Confederate victory.

In one of her letters revealing her frightening racism, she patronizingly wrote of an enslaved African-American. In another she refers to barracks for new African-American soldiers near her home and cruelly ridicules the soldiers.

The following excerpts from Lane's letters are disturbing but reveal her motivation for her support of the Confederacy.

In a long letter written in stages from June 8 to June 16, Lane wrote,

I think if this war goes on everyone will be drawn into it. How can it be otherwise when they now say that Hooker had near 40,000 placed hors de combat in the last battle at Fredericksburg—The loss of life at Vicksburgh is sickening to think of and the end is not yet. It curdles my blood to hear how cooly the deaths of men by the thousand is spoken of, not for the dead, they are happy on any terms to get out of this turmoil, but for the miserable mothers, widows and orphans who are left to weep over this miserable war. Think of 19,000 widows having already claimed pensions and this on one side only, but enough on this subject.

In a passage in the letter dated June 12, she described a visit to the household of a friend.

I found them all very sad at Von Phuls. Fred's youngest child had just died. Eliza has set her heart upon going to Virginia and has applied for a pass. They are all opposed to it for many reasons but cannot bear to contradict her. I said every thing I could against it and told her what I believe is the truth—that if there should be any detention, the anxiety about her would kill her mother. Mrs. MacRee came in while I was there and said more than I dared say for she spoke from sad experience. She told Eliza there was no comfort, no resignation to be hoped for except from time and strict adherence to duty but that it would come. Does it not rather surprise you to hear of Mrs. MacRee being on such a footing in that house—This war has knit the southerners together with closer ties than those of kindred.

A hateful tone permeates the letter when she wrote derisively of the African-Americans who were serving in the Union Army.

Mrs. Brant has started for Texas, when last heard from she was at Helena Such a trip is a terrible undertaking for a woman now—the whole country in that region being filled with soldiers and worse but she had become so anxious about her mother that she resolved to try. She is afraid Mary is dead, otherwise the brother who is in the southern army would have heard from her. If Mrs. B did not— We thought dutch [German] soldiers bad enough but negro ones are worse. The barracks on this street are filled with them dirty ragged with real baboon faces. There is a miserable dirty flag over the building. I thought as I passed it, could a greater insult be offered to the flag enobled by Washington than to hoist it over such a crew? These negroes are as vraie bete noire to me. I think of them the last thing at night and if I am unlucky enough to wake in the night, they are the first thing I remember.

You would laugh if you could see Ally mock the negro sentinels. I sent him to the drug store one evening & he I suppose went on the barracks side of the street, for the darkey ordered him out of the way. He picked up a stick and shewed me with it how the negro handled his gun, hitching along just like Jo, & imitating to the life a negro's voice & manner. A lady who lives on the same square, told me she could compare them to nothing but a menagerie, such yells & screams. Can we sink lower?

In part of the letter dated Tuesday the 16th, she wrote in a patronizing and condescending tone toward Frank, a slave. The letter reveals her own acceptance of slavery.

Frank came home from market this morning considerably stirred up. The recruiting officers are after him constantly, offering to go and bring his wife in &c, &c. He wanted to know of Ma if they could make him go and she told him yes. I told him if he did not want to go, I would spare no pains to save him. He said he did not want to go that his wife was well satisfied and well off and as to their taking care of her, look how they treated the wives of the white soldiers look out for hearing of my being arrested for discouraging enlistments.

Lane mentions "Dick" (Franklin A. Dick) and "Broadhead" (James O. Broadhead), who both served as provost marshal during the war, in a letter dated June 21 and June 27, 1863.

June 21

Mrs. MacRee was here yesterday evening, she has been up before the Provost Martial charged with making disloyal speeches about the time of Camp Jackson & the succeeding summer. She refused to answer any questions but remarked that at that time Americans thought they had a right to say what they thought about every thing. They asked if she was in favor of emancipation in Missouri and if she wished the South crushed out—Nice country this is to live in—If Dick were still Provost—no doubt she would be banished but Broadhead is said to be a decent man. I suppose Drake who has been trying to get some of that ground by law suits failing in that would like to have it confiscated in hopes of coming in for a slice.

In a passage written on June 27, Lane seemed to relish the divisions between the moderate and Unconditional Unionists, hopeful that the division would hand victory to the Confederacy.

The grand inducement to get away from the war is greater than ever. The bitterness is daily becoming more intensifed. Many Union people seeing the Anarchy and ruin to which the country is drifting are getting frightened at what they have helped to do and of course blame the secesh for being the cause of it all. I know for certain that Gamble and his set are thoroughly frightened at the state of things here and are trying their best to stem the radical tide that threatens to sweep over the state. Broadhead's appointment is one step but there are great fears that he will not remain in office. This is neither secesh nor telegraph news so you can depend upon it.

A fragment of letter from 1863 with gossip and family chatter included the following paragraph. She mentions a widowed neighbor, Mrs. O'Flaherty, mother of the feminist writer Kate Chopin. One side of Fourteenth and Papin streets was referred to as Union Row.

Union row was resplendent with one or two dark houses to give releif to the rest. I walked seeing the avenue & all around up here. Frank took the boys down on the cars and shewed them all the sights. He bought Frank G a cockade & a flag and offered one to Allan which was declined. I think Franky was a little ashamed of his for he did not want me to find it on his jacket and gave Sarah the flag who soon tore it up. However, the two Franks went down in great state with their rosettes on their coats. I wish you could have seen Allan's face as he eyed them, but he said nothing—Every thing passed off very quietly—the only outrage I heard was the soldiers going in to Mrs. O'Flaherty's on 8 St. near Chouteau Ave. breaking the vases in her yard and the Shrubbery & hoisting a flag over her house. To my amazement the barracks where the darkeys are was not illumined.

Amongst gossip and references to acquaintances staying in Europe, the following paragraph concluded by addressing a fear of many young American ladies.

Kate Shea is married so our girls say—a match of Margaret's making—This man refused to marry her after the bans were published but afterwards Margaret coaxed him to marry her. I hope she has done well, maybe she was in a hurry fearing men would be scarce if the war went on.

William Carr Lane Papers, Missouri History Museum Archives.

Julia Dent Grant

J ulia Dent Grant recalled staying with her father at White Haven in South County during the summer of 1863. She wrote about her Southern-sympathizing neighbors and about the way she received the long-awaited news that Vicksburg had surrendered to her husband, General Ulysses S. Grant.

My summer was not a happy one. Our neighbors were all Southern in sentiment and could not believe that I was not; no matter how earnestly I denied it, they would exclaim: "It is right for you to say you are Union, Julia, but we know better, my child; it is not in human nature for you to be anything but Southern." They would imprudently speak of mails going to the South from various places, and when I remonstrated with them, saying, "I might feel it my duty to repeat these things to the authorities," they would smile and say, "We know you will not. We know how you have been brought up and an oath would not be more binding than the sanctity of your roof." We enjoyed the country greatly: the lofty trees, the singing birds, and my dear father's society. He argued and ar- gued with me constantly upon the constitutionality of secession. I was dreadfully puzzled about the horrid old Constitution anyway . . .

One afternoon early in July, as we were sitting in an upper room chatting, we were interrupted by a perfect salvo of artillery. I started up much excited and called down from my window to papa, who sat on the piazza reading the papers, asking what he supposed the matter was; if he thought Vicksburg had surrendered. "Yes, I should not wonder if both Vicksburg and Richmond had fallen from the infernal noise they are making." But dear papa was always pleased at any success of my husband and was immensely proud of him, notwithstanding his great sympathy with the South. Soon a courier arrived with the news of the surrender and with an invitation for myself and family to go to St. Louis to witness the grand parade in honor of the great victory of Grant, but I did not go. . . . In a few days, however, one of General Grant's staff officers, Major [William M.] Dunn, arrived at Cairo, and, after telegraphing the glorious news to the Secretary of War, was privately directed to come to St. Louis and to escort the children and me to Vicksburg to visit General Grant.

After recalling the fall of Vicksburg, Julia related an oft-repeated, but unconfirmed, story of Lincoln's response to complaints that General Grant drank.

President Lincoln, who, on being importuned to relieve General Grant for his intemperance, anxiously inquired, "Do you know what brand of whiskey Grant drinks? I would like to get barrels of it and send to my other generals."

Julia Dent Grant, The Personal Memoirs of Julia Dent Grant *(Carbondale: Southern Illinois University Press, 1975), 113-14.*

EDWARD BATES

The yard of the Union Iron Works at Carondelet was the scene of celebration at the launching of the iron gunboat *Winnebago* on July 4, 1863.

The self-taught river engineer, James B. Eads, had leased the boatyard in the neighboring river city of Carondelet, then south of the city of St. Louis, to build mortar rafts and ironclad gunboats. Ulysses S. Grant used these ironclads at Forts Henry and Donelson and to conquer Vicksburg.

Carloads of people and boatloads of passengers had traveled to the ironworks to take part in the Independence Day launching. The ceremonies included U.S. Attorney General Edward Bates, who called St. Louis home, presenting a flag to Eads. While he spoke, Vicksburg was falling into federal hands, and word was spreading about a great battle that had just concluded at Gettysburg.

Bates's words are resolute.

Friends and Fellow-Citizens: I feel particularly gratified to meet my old and true friend J.B. Eads, and honored in being present on this occasion. In being amongst you, I feel like returning home after an absence of two or three years—a home endeared to me by all the recollections of fifty years, for it is fifty years since I first arrived at St. Louis. I come amongst you upon an occasion dear to my heart, because it is valuable to my country. I am not come here to make a Fourth of July speech; I have done that oftentimes before; but I have come expressly honored by an invitation from these worthy men who have served their country so well, and who, by their skill and industry in building these noble but terrible engines of war, are preparing the way for the re-establishment of peace, order and law. I come here by invitation of the noble men of this yard, to testify for them their respectful regard and favor for the worthy head of this noble yard, my old friend Eads. These noble and patriotic workmen have asked me to present to their worthy head a token of their respect and regard in the shape of the banner of their country; there it lies, the emblem of our obedience, and of our country's sovereignty and power, the flag under which our brave soldiers are marching to victory, honor and peace.

I said I was not going to make a Fourth of July speech, nevertheless I cannot forget it is the cherished day of our country's independence. We cannot, if we would, forget the recollection of those high, holy and hallowed thoughts, connected with this most precious day. We cannot forget that this is the day on which our ancestors stood united and firm against the then most powerful nation on the globe, and that remembrance should serve to excite our best feelings, and animate our highest hopes, and cheer us on in our struggle against our present foes—though they are of our own people—who would divide and desolate our land. It has been my fortune to witness some of the scenes, and to have the cares and fears of many more detailed to me, of the calamities of this cruel civil war. It has been my fortune to see the wealthy reduced to necessity, and to see a large portion of our country torn and desolated with blood, and you, my friends, you, are among those who serve your country as effectually by the faithful discharge of your duty in these and similar works, as do those gallant and glorious men, who fight, bleed and die in our country's battles.

This place is our home, though, perhaps, some have immigrated from other places, but this place in which we stand is connected with all our associations of power, wealth and intelligence that are to strengthen and adorn this land. We stand at the centre of the wonderful Mississippi, in the great central valley of this nation. You stand in the midst of 25,000 miles of natural navigation. Boats have been launched from this yard that can penetrate the various waters of the Mississippi for 25,000 miles; spanning the continent east, west, north and south. Western Pennsylvania is in the Valley of the Mississippi; the gorges of the Rocky Mountains are in the Valley of the Mississippi, and from the Osage we can run to either extremity.

After discussing the vastness of the Mississippi River Valley, and recalling that twelve years earlier, at the commencement of the Pacific Railroad, the nation needed no army, Bates returned to the subject of that day in the boat yard.

Now we have other and more arduous duties to perform. Now is the deadly struggle for a nation's life, and we must either conquer or die. No nation, no people on the earth, ever willingly committed suicide. They die, if die they must, in convulsive agonies, struggling to the last for existence. All the efforts carried on so successfully thus far, in this navy yard, are intended to accomplish the destruction of the power that has arisen against us, to subdue all opposition and reestablish the institutions of our forefathers.

I have conversed not only with statesmen, but with some of the ablest and best of our naval commanders with reference to the building and fitting of gunboats for the Mississippi river. The idea of a gunboat on the waters of the Mississippi was a novelty; some ridiculed it; but some few of the naval officers sincerely believed in the possibility of the thing, and saw in it, as clearly as sunlight could have revealed the fact, and all powerful, all conquering instrument for crushing the rebellion and for the support of the institutions of our forefathers.

This yard established for building gunboats, was an experiment, hazardous alike to the treasury of the nation, and to the reputation for skill and knowledge of the excellent and able man involved in it, was taken first of all by my friend James B. Eads, under a contract with Government to build seven steamers, and under the command of that noble and glorious man, whom I might well be proud to call my friend, but who has left us, and is gone to receive the rich reward that awaited him; who has entered into blessed communion with the spirits of the just made perfect; Admiral Foote is dead, but he still lives in the hearts of his countrymen. . . .

What would have been your condition upon the Ohio, but for the gunboats of the Mississippi? What would have taken Fort Henry, Fort Donelson and Columbus? Without them our armies would have been inefficient, and the enemy this day would have domineered over the whole course of the Mississippi, . . .

Such is the high vocation held by you, from the head of this yard, and the able and excellent officers of the Government who superintend and control its direction—down to each individual workman—the safety and integrity of the nation; and there is, I feel confident, not a man in this yard who is not persuaded of the importance of his position, and of the glorious work he is performing.

But I must come to the point—to the honor for which I was called here. Not only in response to your kind invitation, but by strong sympathy, and by close friendship for my worthy and esteemed friend, Eads. . . . Our object in being here is to present, as a gift of respect and honor, from the gentlemen of this yard to their worthy head, Mr. Eads, the glorious flag of their country. There it lies, trussed up in excellent form—as our old salts know so well how to do. My old friend Eads, in the name of these excellent and respectable men, who have long served faithfully under you, and serving you, have served faithfully their country, in their name, and in mutual honor of you and them, I present that Flag—the flag of our country, the adored flag of our nation. There it lies, silent, quiet and modest now; it is only when there is occasion for it that it floats in the face of the enemy, and brings dire destruction on all who assail it. I beg that honored flag may now seek its proper element and be raised to its proper place.

The *Missouri Republican* reported that three cheers were given as Bates assisted in raising the flags. There were even more enthusiastic cheers as the flag floated in the breeze. Eads then made a speech that concluded,

Gentlemen of the Union Iron Works, you have given me a splendid present; it is a noble banner; it is worth toiling for, fighting for, and dying for. [Loud cheers.] When I see its ample folds spread to the breeze my heart will swell within me at the thoughts that so many warm friends are laboring to the end that it may wave in triumph over an undivided land; [cheers] and I pledge you, Mr. Attorney General, that the men of the Union Iron Works will not cease to labor with the same zeal and patriotic devotion which they have thus far shown, till that banner is respected from the lakes to the gulf, from ocean to ocean. [Cries of that's so, and cheers.] My friends of the Iron Works, while your gift is floating on the breeze, let us adorn the old Father of floods with the present from the Union Iron Works; let us give to his bosom the Iron Clad Winnebago!

The crowd gave three hearty cheers for Captain Eads, three more for Attorney General Bates, and three more for Captain W. S. Wilson, superintendent of the works, according to the *Republican*. Then the crowd rushed to obtain favorable views of the launch. Those with tickets, including General John Schofield, hurried to the deck of the *Winnebago*.

At each prop that supported the vessel, one workman stood with a sledge in hand. At a given signal, they knocked the marine props from under the boat, and after a pause, the ponderous, floating fortification rushed from its inclined bed into the Mississippi, amid the waving of flags and shouts of thousand of interested spectators.

Missouri Republican, *July 5, 1863.*

DAILY MISSOURI DEMOCRAT

REPORTS ON HYDE PARK RIOT

A local Independence Day celebration proved a sad backdrop for the news of armies waging fierce battles. Festivities scheduled for Hyde Park attracted mobs of soldiers, many convalescing. The crowds—plus plentiful drink—added to ongoing hostilities with local Confederate sympathizers. This combination of drink and tensions erupted into waves of fights and riots. Police and troops were overwhelmed. Finally, the troops fired into the crowds. Citizens and soldiers were wounded, and some killed.

While the papers carried news of the disgraceful violence in a local park, they also carried news of Vicksburg and Gettysburg. It was several days before the stories of Vicksburg's surrender was confirmed in the papers. News from Gettysburg was also slow, and at first misleading, with newspapers falsely reporting that Confederate General James Longstreet had been killed.

As the news of the major battles trickled in, outraged St. Louisans debated and discussed the riot in the park. The *Missouri Republican* of Tuesday Morning, July 7, 1863, editorialized on the "Row at Hyde Park" and the appropriateness of liquor served in public parks. "Hyde Park belongs to the city. It was purchased for a most excellent object, as a breathing place for the women and children of that section of the city, and would have been appropriated in that way if it had not been for the cupidity of the City Council. . . ." Then it was converted into "a place of public resort, where refreshments could be obtained by all classes of people, and the original object was lost sight of."

"We say it is the City Fathers, who, disregarding their duty, and pandering to a depraved taste, perverted this property from its appropriate use, and almost insured these abominations."

Accounts of the celebration erupting into violence were confusing and varied radically. The *Daily Missouri Democrat* carried a lengthy description of the events on July 6. Even though wrinkles in the newspaper make a few occasional paragraphs unreadable, this account clearly reports on the waves of violence throughout the day. Spelling, style, and some words in this article are antiquated.

FOURTH OF JULY TRAGEDY AT HYDE PARK.

Immense Crowd-A Wild Riot—The Rioters Fired Upon—
Innocent Persons Killed.

A series of aggravated disturbances, resulting in the immediate killing of five persons, and the wounding of about a dozen others, some of them fatally, disgraced the afternoon of the Fourth, at Hyde Park.

Extensive preparations had been made by the lessee of the Park, Mr. Kuhlage, to attract thither crowds of men, women and children for the enjoyment of the national festival, and multitudes flocked to the place. Among them came large throngs of soldiers, principally paroled Union prisoners, from Benton Barracks. Their officers had given them the day for recreation, and they were bent upon making the most of it. It is not true, as has been reported, that they came to the Park with arms, except so far as, like other citizens, they may have had knives or pistols concealed on the person. Nor does it appear that they were intoxicated when entering the Park. The cause and the occasien of the subsequent difficulties so far as we could learn them, are about as follows:

Among the soldiers of Benton Barracks, or a considerable portion of them, had sprung up a feeling inimical to Mr. Kuhlage, they accusing him of being a secessionist refusing to hoist the national flag till compelled &c., &c.. The Park being in the neighborhood of the Barracks, soldiers were frequently calling there for beer, and occasional difficulties occurred to aggravate the animosity. It is alleged that, when out of funds, some of the paroled soldiers persistently drank and failed to pay. It is also averred that, in view of the feeling of certain soldiers and in consequence of their threats, numbers of citizens refrained from visiting the Park on the Fourth, through apprehensions of a riot. On that day, however, affairs there seemed progressing as smoothly as could be reasonably desired until about 2 p.m.

By that hour, the beer and other liquors furnished at the place, having flowed copiously, produced their natural effect, rendering hundreds noisy and excitable, and producing frequent but comparatively harmless altercations. At the front gate much disturbance arose from the numbers crowding for admittance, while the entrance was narow, and the slow process of ticketing was adhered to. Reckless youths, and bad "boys of larger grewth" forced ingress from all quarters by tearing off boards from the fence. A force of policemen was sent for, but order was restored by District Provost Marshal Allen, who was opportunely on the ground, and who stationed a half dozen guards of the 2d Missouri Artillery [a company of whom were quartered within the enclosure] at the front gate. Soon after 3 p.m. a violent quarrel arose in the bar-room in the east end of Kuhlage's house, from the bar-keeper not returning, in one instance, the amount or change claimed. Becoming fearful of a riot, Mr. K. refused to sell any more beer to the applicants, who were thus only the worse incensed. The bar-keeper was so hardly pressed, and so impudent that he suddenly drew both a pistol and a bowie knife and with the latter cut a soldier in the arm. This was the signal for a general onset upon the establishment, the barkeeper and other employees, with soda and wine bottles, boxes, chairs, benches, rocks and every other missile available. The barkeeper and those with him were completely overpowered, but escaped with bruised persons and torn clothes, while the work of destruction went on till almost everything frangible was smashed. Doors were stoven in, window sash and glass broken, counters overtuned and wrecked, shelves torn down, furniture shattered, stoves kicked over, pantries demolished, and the dining room and parlor sacked, while little and ineffective opposition was made. Consternation seized the peaceful visitors at the tables in the grove, and a multitude of frightened men, women and children rushed "helter-skelter" for the gate. Fair ones and weak ones were threwn down in the crowd and several narrowly missed being trampled to death. The police and guards, however, kept back the crowd in time to prevent such disaster. Captain Allen hastened to the scene of strife at the first outbreak, and sought to employ a force of the artillery company referred to, but the men failed to recognize his authority, their Captain was not at hand, and they refused to "Go in." Taking, however, three of the guard from the gate, he led them with presented bayonets to the spot, and succeeded at last in quelling this disturbance. Meanwhile a policeman had attacked and kicked one of the rioters, who soon after returned upon him; but the officer was aided by a person who charged the disturber with stealing a coat on which the "star" took the accused in custody and began walking with him toward the gate. Two military officers attended the policeman, and protected him from the crowd that thronged to effect a rescue. A "big bully" at length interfered and "pitched into" the policeman, who was compelled to let the prisoner go and defend himself. While doing this he found himself falling into a perilous minority and concluded to retreat. Exhibiting a pistol to keep his adversaries at bay, he made fleet steps from the premises. Another policeman fared worse, and only escaped after very rough usage. The reinforcement of "stars" sent for arrived, but numbered only some fifteen, and being without muskets, could effect little. Mr. Kuhlage and family improved the earliest opportunity to leave the establishment, which had now no other protection than the few guards and police could give.

After the restoration of quiet, things continued measurably tranquil till about 5 o'clock, when another cause of dissatisfaction appeared in the failure of the greatly advertised balloon to realize the anticipations excited. The hour of its ascension had long passed, and the protracted efforts to patch it and fill it excited the derision of the crowd. Added was the irritating fact that hundreds had each paid fifty cents to "see the balloon and horse go up," while hundreds of others enjoyed equal facilities even if the ascension should take place, by having paid an admission fee of only 25 cents. Besides many declared that the Park belonged to the city, and that the lessee was prohibited from ever asking any admission fee. . . .

Though much of the next section of the account is unreadable, there are references to a crowd rushing the partly filled balloon, and fireworks being "let off."

The fireworks were summarily made a bonfire of, going off with a brilliant rapidity, rarely achieved in pyrotechnics. All this was done in three or four minutes. The rioters next made a rush for Kuhlage's house, to extend if possible, the work of destruction already wrought there.

At this instant was heard the long roll beating to quarters the soldiers of Captain Lauman company, 2d Missouri Artillery, located in the rear of the house and the north end of the park. . . .

In another mostly unreadable section, there are references indicating the troops fired into a crowd.

A portion of the weapons were directed towards the southeast and others discharged in a southwesterly direction. The crowd east, ran and that part of the field was cleared, but exhibited no person fallen or wounded. It is claimed that the Lieutenant ordered the men to fire with blank cartridges only, and this order may have been to some extent obeyed, but bullets were distinctly heard whistling over the heads of this crowd.

In the other direction five persons were shot fatally. One was outside of the Park on the west of it. A ball passed through his head, killing him almost instantly. He was one of the paroled soldiers. Two others, also paroled soldiers were shot down. One had a portion of his forehead and skull removed. He was afterward lifted, apparently dead, into a soda wagon and carried off. It is not since learned whither the body was taken, but no doubt is entertained of his death. A third was instantly killed by a ball shot through his person, entering at about the middle of the back. It is ascertained that his name is J. M. Smith, and that he was a private in Company B, 3rd Mo. volunteers.

A young man of sixteen years, named Louis Francis Demette, a Frenchman, was instantly shot dead, the ball entering the back of the head and passing out at the right eye. He resided with his widowed mother at the corner of Broadway and Palm streets, and was her sole support as well as that of his younger brothers and sisters.

Another young man, by the name of Henry Nieters, aged sixteen years and a half, was similarly killed. The bullet entered the forehead and lodged in the lower portion of the back of the head. The youth sank and at once expired. He had just been conversing with a young man of his own age who had accompanied him to the Park, and who urged him to immediately leave. He declined, saying "Let's go and see what's the matter!" The other left, and Nieters proceeded a few steps after the charging soldiers, when the fatal ball pierced him. He was an orphan, a native of St. Louis, and employed by Mr. Siemers, jeweler, on the South side of Franklin avenue, between Fifth and Sixth streets, by whom he had been reared and as highly esteemed.

Among the wounded was James Odell, laborer, who received a bayonet cut in the head, another in the leg and a third in the breast, besides being badly beaten with the butt of a musket. We do not learn what provocation, if any, he had given. He lies at his residence on the west side of 6th street, between O'Fallon street and Cass avenue.

Michael Banier, a youth of seventeen years, was wounded while standing at the front gate of the Park. The ball struck and broke his leg. He was picked up and conveyed to his home at Ninth and Wash streets, where amputation had to be performed.

A soldier of the 29th Missouri, who was on guard at the front gate, had his leg broken in like manner. He was taken to his quarters at Benton Barracks.

A woman whose name is not learned, received a severe wound in the mouth; Other persons whose names do not transpire, left or were carried from the ground with injuries of a less serious nature.

At about 11 o'clock Saturday night the Coroner held brief inquest, at Hyde Park, upon the bodies of Nieters and Demette, arriving in each instance at the conclusion that deceased had been murderously shot by a person or persons unknown to the jury. The name of Nieters could not be learned at the inquest upon him.

An inquest will to-day be held at Smither's Undertaker's shop, on Chestnut street, on the body of J.M. Smith. It is to be hoped that time and care will be taken to get impartial and intelligent witnesses, whose combined testimony will place the facts of this sad tragedy in their true light. Extreme statements are current for and against the action of the soldiers in firing, and only the patient collection of details personally known to individuals, and the examination of their evidence can satisfactorily show where the truth lies.

After noting the extreme and contradictory statements about the riot, the last paragraph of the article described the epilogue.

At six o'clock yesterday morning [July 5] a party of marauders and despoilers entered the deserted park and resumed the work of destroying what they could break. They helped themselves freely to the liquors remaining in casks, and actually rolled away without hindrance certain barrels of whisky from the premises. This conduct was in the vein of that the previous day, when an entire load of lager casks were seized and drank. Yesterday noon District Provost Marshal Allen ordered Capt. Brown of the Provost Guard, to send twenty-five men, mounted if practicable, to take possession of the park, and keep off the thieves and malicious destroyers. At 6 pm the guard was relieved by police and a guard from the company of Capt Lauman.

Daily Missouri Democrat, *July 6, 1863*.

Sarah Full Hill

When James B. Eads leased the boatyard in the neighboring river city of Carondelet, now the southernmost neighborhood of the city of St. Louis, to build mortar rafts and ironclad gunboats, the little city boomed. With Carondelet's boatyard bustling with industry, a housing shortage near the yard resulted. Hill's mother needed income and recognized the opportunity offered in Carondelet.

Some old and influential friends of my father came to Mother and asked her to take charge and manage a house where these men [officials with the boatyard] could have a congenial home and be together. There was a large house on the bluff overlooking the works and the river, about five minutes walk from the yards. It was a stately old mansion of former days, surrounded by orchards and beautiful grounds. It was now vacant and the place was falling into disrepair. The owner and the family were living in the South, but the twenty room house was an ideal one for the purpose contemplated.

Some of the friends who were interesting Mother in the project had large contracts with the government for iron and steel and materials for the building of the gunboats, and they had thought it a fine opportunity for Mother, as well as making living conditions more pleasant for the working officials in whom they were interested. They promised to put the interior of the house in living repair and to keep the house full of paying guests, Mother to furnish the house and help and to have all the proceeds. If Mother needed help to start, they would loan her the money. We hesitated and thought the matter over. I wrote E.M. on the subject. He thought

Mother had the ability to manage such an establishment and said we would finance her, so she would not have to borrow money outside or pay interest.

Mother decided to accept the proposition and moved down to the place in March. She had much furniture of her own, and bought comfortable furnishings for the many bedrooms. She retained two rooms and a parlor on the ground floor for herself and family. When the house opened, twenty-seven men engaged board and rooms, and many more wanted to come, but the house was filled.

Now began busy days for the family. The greatest difficulty which we encountered was in procuring and keeping help. It was so far from the city and town they would not stay, but Mother and the two older girls and myself were healthy and strong and we were not afraid to work. In one of the Negro cabins on the place lived the Negro caretaker and his wife, old slaves of the family. He took care of the garden and the cow, and his wife did the laundry work and scrubbing at the "big house." It was a delightful place in many ways, and our little ones, Mother's two little girls and my little boy, spent most of their days out of doors in the old orchard and grew so rosy and strong and were no care. Indeed, we were all very happy and busy and glad to be out of the city, and Mother was prospering and she enjoyed catering for the gentlemen who were her guests.

The booming economy and demand for housing in Carondelet was short-lived. When Sarah returned to Carondelet after a lengthy stay in Vicksburg,

A sad state of affairs was revealed. When getting off the train at the little station, I had noticed the shipyards were partially closed and very few men seemed to be about. There was no clink clank of hammers, no pounding of iron and steel, an unusual quiet seemed to pervade the place. I asked the station agent about it. He said the government had stopped building the river gunboats since the river was open to navigation and only kept a small force of men there to repair the boats of the fleet that were used as patrols. That meant trouble for Mother.

On reaching the house I found poor Mother and her four girl children entirely alone in that great barn of a place . . .

Hill, 154-158, 199.

JOSEPH A. FARDELL
THE INVALID CORPS
AT JEFFERSON BARRACKS HOSPITAL

In the spring and summer of 1863, Joseph A. Fardell of Company C, 131st Illinois Volunteers, was a patient at Jefferson Barracks General Hospital. While there, he was assigned to the U.S. Veterans Reserve Corps, also know as the Invalid Corps. Its two battalions were made up of men who, by reason of wound or disease, were unfit for combat service. They could, however, perform behind-the-lines duties, such as clerical and hospital service, which freed healthier men for combat duty.

In his letters to his parents—Mr. and Mrs. F. S. Shanks, who lived in Pope County, Illinois—Fardell provided updates on his health and gave a detailed accounting of his chores while in the Invalid Corps.

Fardell's phonetic spelling and lack of punctuation suggests he had little formal education, or that he had attended a Blab School, where due to lack of books, the students learned from recitation.

July 11, 1863

. . . as to my helth it is good. it is as good as it ever has been in the army I am almost as Stout as I ever Was in life though I am not fit for field Duty nor never will be. . . . I am in this Invalid Corps So I expect to serve my time out in this or sum other Hosp. . . . Mother you need not think because I am in a Hospital that I am sick all the time for I am not everyone that is here is not sick though they may have sum Disaes that may render them unfit for field service and at the same time be able to do as much here as if they was perfeckly well. . . .

August 9, 1863

. . . I am in the Invilid Corps . . . it would be foolishness for me to leve this place and go to the Co. but it would Suit me as I am not content here I dount like to Stay in one place So long. . . . I will give you a full history of What I have to do here and probably you can give me Some advise on the Subject in the first place I have left the Drugstore that I was in I now have charge of the Stewards Mess Which is in Hosp No 1 Mess No 2 there is 4 Wardmasters 2 Stewards 2 Druggists and 4 Lady Nurses making in all 12 in the Mess to cook for and thare is three hands beside me to do this cooking all I hafto do is to bake the Cakes and pies Which is onely done twist a Week and onely takes 1/2 of a day each time Which is Wednesday and Saterday I have as good [a] bed to Sleep in as you have and just as much to eat as the Country affords all I hafto do is just What I have told. . . .

The Jefferson Barracks Notebook, Jefferson Barracks Park Archives.

William Greenleaf Eliot

William Geenleaf Eliot was born in 1811 in New Bedford, Massachusetts, and moved to St. Louis in 1834 after graduatng from the Harvard Divinity School. He established the first Unitarian Church west of the Mississippi. He was founder and later chancellor of Washington University and was instrumental in the operations of the Western Sanitary Commission. His letters show his care to details and how he encouraged individuals in their goodness and generosity.

On Western Sanitary Commission letterhead, he wrote the following letter to young donors, Miss Abbie and Kitty Alger, on March 7, 1863.

My dear girls.

Your ten handkerchiefs were received only a few days ago, because it has taken longer than usual for boxes to come this last month. It is a great comfort to the sick men to have plenty of handkercheifs. To-day I was with a young man, only 16 yrs old, who was wounded nine months ago, and is only just now getting well! What a long time that is, to be sick & suffering in hospital.

We thank you for your kind gift, and you must think of me as your

Sincere friend
<u>W.G. Eliot</u>

In this undated letter, Eliot involves the donors, Abbie Alger and Lucy Jackson, to help decide how their gift should be spent. In listing how financial gifts could be used, Eliot left a record of the needs of the soldiers.

My dear Girls.

I have received your money, $1.98, and thank you very much.

Now what shall I do with it? I can think of a good many things, but can't quite make up my mind. It would buy a nice warm flannel shirt for some sick soldier. Or I could buy a big turkey, enough for a New Year's day dinner for nine or ten men, at the soldiers home. Or, it would get twelve copies of the New Testament, for twelve soldiers on their way to fight for our country. Or, it would supply eight pocket-handkercheifs. What <u>shall</u> I do? Please write to me just a few words, and then I shall know just what to buy. Or perhaps you would like me to send it directly to General Grant, or General Sherman, and tell them just how you earned it, and ask them to give it with their own hands to some brave boy.

I shall wait till I hear from you, before I spend it and remain

Your Sincere Friend
<u>W.G. Eliot</u>

Breckenridge files, Missouri History Museum Archives.

James E. Yeatman, George Partridge, John B. Johnson, Carlos S. Greeley, and William G. Eliot

L eaders of the Western Sanitary Commission lobbied President Abraham Lincoln for permission to serve the "Freed Negroes," in the Southwest and South. Their letter addressed the heartbreaking conditions of the freed slaves, and the large numbers throughout the Mississippi Valley needing help. The signers included Unitarian Minister William Greenleaf Eliot; reformed slave owner James E. Yeatman; physician John B. Johnson; and grocers George Partridge and Carlos Greeley. Their letter reflected the great generosity and spirit of these St. Louisans and the many volunteers who were the backbone of their organization.

Letter to the President of the United States.
Rooms Western Sanitary Commission,
St. Louis, November 6th, 1863

His Excellency, A. Lincoln,
President of the United States

Sir:—

The undersigned, members of the Western Sanitary Commission, most respectfully represent, that the condition of the Freed Negroes in the Mississippi Valley is daily becoming worse, and calls most loudly upon the humane and loyal people of the Northern States for help. There are probably not less than fifty thousand, chiefly women and children, now within our lines, between Cairo and New Orleans, for whom no adequate provision has been made. The majority of them have no shelter but what they call "brush tents," fit for nothing but to protect them from night dews. They are very poorly clad—many of them half naked—and almost destitute of beds and bedding—thousands of them sleeping on the bare ground. The Government supplies them with *rations*, but many unavoidable delays arise in the distribution, so that frequent instances of great destitution occur. The army rations (beef and crackers) are also a kind of diet they are not used to; they have no facilities of cooking, and are almost ignorant of the use of wheat flour; and even when provisions in abundance are supplied, they are so spoiled in cooking as to be neither eatable nor wholesome. Add to these difficulties, the helplessness and improvidence of those who have always been slaves, together with their forlorn and jaded condition when they reach our lines, and we can easily account for the fact that sickness and death prevail to a fearful extent. No language can describe the suffering, destitution and neglect which prevail in some of their "camps." The sick and dying are left uncared for, in many instances, and the dead unburied. It would seem, now, that one-half are doomed to die in the process of freeing the rest.

Our purpose is not to find fault, but to seek for the remedy. Undoubtedly, Congress must take the matter in hand, to mature plans of permanent relief; but, judging from past experience, a good many months will elapse before its final action, and there will still remain a great deal that properly belongs to private charity, and for which legislation cannot provide.

To meet the present exigency, and to prevent or lessen the sufferings of the coming winter and spring, we offer our humble but active services, asking no reward of any kind, but the opportunity and encouragement to work. Our experience for two and a-half years past, in the sanitary cause of the sick and wounded, has taught us the lessons of economy and prudence, and we are too much accustomed to difficulties to be discouraged by them. . . . that in the two years from October, 1861, to November, 1863, we have received and expended for the sick and wounded of the Western Army, in stores or money, to the amount of a million and a quarter of dollars, and that the total expenses of distribution, including all salaries and incidental charges, has been but little in excess of *one per cent.* [The commissioners offered as references for their work and good results Generals Grant, Sherman, Schofield, Fremont, Halleck, and others.]

We now respectfully ask permission and authority to extend our labors to the suffering freed people of the South-West and South. . . . Nor would it be only a work of philanthropy, but equally of patriotism, for it would remove an increasing reproach against the Union cause, and by lessening the difficulties of emancipation, would materially aid in crushing the rebellion. At present, hundreds of the blacks would gladly return to slavery, to avoid the hardships of freedom; and if this feeling increases and extends itself among them, all the difficulties of the situation will be increased; while, at the same time, a most effective argument is given to the disloyal against our cause.

We most respectfully leave the subject before you, feeling sure that you will agree with us as to the necessity of prompt and energetic action, And have the honor to remain,

Your cordial friends and obedient servants,

James E. Yeatman,
George Partridge,
John B. Johnson,
Carlos S. Greeley,
William G. Eliot.

William Greenleaf Eliot Papers, Missouri History Museum Archives.

1864

"Dire calamities remain"
—*Louis Philip Fusz*

The year brought shattering losses on the battlefield. Yet two Union generals with ties to St. Louis devised and executed strategies that would defeat the South. On March 2, local farmer Ulysses S. Grant was confirmed by the U.S. Senate as lieutenant general, the first since George Washington, and took command of the largest army in the world, soon to number a million men. During 1864, Grant fought Lee and his army south, through the horrors of the battles of the Wilderness and Cold Harbor. He kept pushing Lee back toward Richmond. The man who had been running 5th Street Railway in St. Louis when the war began, William Tecumseh Sherman, led the Union Armies of the West. They fought Confederate Armies from Chattanooga to Atlanta.

When the year began, St. Louis secessionists stilled dreamed of success. When the year ended, even the most stalwart secessionists in St. Louis recognized their defeat as inevitable.

While young men from St. Louis were fighting on both sides in these campaigns, the local Union community and Confederate sympathizers became more and more polarized.

Perhaps the only thing they shared was the bitter cold of the winter of 1864. A storm with fierce winds had drifted the snow. Streetcars and traffic were stopped. The Mississippi froze over, the thick ice providing a smooth path for men, sleighs, and heavy wagons from St. Louis to the Illinois shoreline. Tents and temporary structures were built on the ice. One of the ramshackle structures was named the Lindell Hotel on the Ice, after the glamorous Lindell Hotel on Washington Avenue.

The community held an elegant celebration that bitter January, in honor of Ulysses S. Grant and other Union generals. As the war continued, the waves of convalescing soldiers and refugees taxed the generosity of

St. Louisans. By May 1, the number of patients treated in the hospitals of St. Louis, including Jefferson Barracks and Benton Barracks, was 61,744. Volunteers planned and conducted an enormous fair to raise funds for the Western Sanitary Commission and its work among the wounded and refugees.

In some ways, day-to-day life possessed a normalcy. Men went to work in the iron foundries and commission houses. Women did the laundry, paid higher prices at the stores, and worked at the military hospitals. The draft continued to call up more young men to fill the ranks in the Union Army.

Remarkably, Saint Louis University began construction of a new building, four stories tall and measuring eighty-by-eighty feet, at Washington Avenue and Ninth Street. With ten classrooms, a dormitory, and the Philalethic Hall, it was ready to use for the fall semester.

Local secessionists muffled their feelings, which sometimes became more hateful. The threat of being drafted for the Union Army spurred some to flee to the Confederate Armies. Despite their devastating defeats at Gettysburg and Vicksburg the previous year, the secessionists saw hope in every loss they inflicted on the Union. They hung their dreams on the presidential election of 1864, confident Democratic candidate General George McClellan could defeat Lincoln, and sue for peace. When Robert E. Lee and his Army of Northern Virginia stalled Grant outside of Petersburg, and General John Hood commanding the Armies of Tennessee and Mississippi stalled Sherman's Army at Atlanta, the hopes of Confederates swelled.

Then Phil Sheridan's campaign through the Shenandoah Valley and Sherman's Army, including many St. Louisans, taking Atlanta on September 2, buoyed the Union and changed the political climate.

While Sherman led his Western Army through the South, and Grant hammered the Army of Northern Virginia, St. Louis and all of Missouri was threatened again. Confederate General Sterling Price led a tired force of twelve thousand troops into Missouri on September 19. He hoped that the Confederate guerrilla forces across the state would rise up and support him. He also knew that though St. Louis was a major staging area for the war, since the war had swept south, the city was left largely unprotected. Union General William Rosecrans hurriedly threw up defenses around St. Louis. However, Union General Thomas Ewing with one thousand men, half of them green recruits, repelled Confederate assaults at Fort Davidson eighty-five miles south of St. Louis. After causing heavy casualties, Ewing and his forces slipped away. Price turned toward Jefferson City, where seventy-two hundred entrenched Federals repelled them. The great uprising of secessionists did not materialize. A series of battles and skirmishes continued, until Price and the Confederates were finally pushed back along the Missouri-Kansas border all the way to the Arkansas River. The last threat to St. Louis had ended.

In November, Lincoln won with 55 percent of the popular vote. The polling place had unmistakably demonstrated the determination of the people of the Union to win the war. Local secessionists lost hope. The inevitability of Union victory led some St. Louisans to talk of emigrating to Mexico.

After weeks of being out of communication, Sherman's Western Army of sixty-two thousand men emerged at Savannah before Christmas. The huge army had marched from Atlanta to the sea, plundering, wreaking havoc, and erasing the South's ability to wage war.

ANN VALENTINE

ince the Emancipation Proclamation freed only slaves in Confederate states, the circumstances of African-Americans in Missouri continued to be filled with uncertainty and hardship. James A. Carney of Paris, Missouri, wrote a letter on behalf of an enslaved woman that reflects the terrifying situation for one African-American family.

Husband and father, Andrew Valentine, served in the Union Armies, while his enslaved family was at the mercy of their owner. Carney wrote this letter for Ann to her husband in the 2nd Missouri Colored Infantry stationed in St. Louis's Benton Barracks. Ann told Carney what she wanted to write to her husband and at the end, Carney added directions on how Valentine could best communicate with his wife in the future.

Paris Mo Jany 19, 1864

My Dear Husband I r'ecd your letter dated Jan'y 9th also one dated Jany 1 but have got no one till now to write for me. You do not know how bad I am treated. They are treating me worse and worse every day. Our child cries for you. Send me some money as soon as you can for me and my child are almost naked. My cloth is yet in the loom and there is no telling when it will be out. Do not send any of your letters to Hogsett [her owner] especially those having money in them as Hogsett will keep the money. George Combs went to Hannibal soon after you did so I did not get that money from him. Do the best you can and do not fret too much for me for it wont be long before I will be free and then all we make will be ours. Your affectionate wife

Ann

P.S. Sind our little girl a string of beads in your next letter to remember you by. Ann

Andy if you send me any more letters for your wife do not send them in the care of any one. Just direct them plainly to James A Carney Paris Monroe County Mo. Do not write too often Once a month will be plenty and when you write do not write as though you had recd any letters for if you do your wife will not be so apt to get them. Hogsett has forbid her coming to my house so we cannot read them to her privately. If you send any money I will give that to her myself. Yrs & c

Jas A Carney

Ira Berlin, editor, Freedom: A Documentary History of Emancipation, Series II *(London: Cambridge University Press, 1982).*

LOUIS PHILIP FUSZ

In this divided city, Unconditional Unionists and devoted secessionists often shared the same pew in church. While attending Catholic
Mass, Louis Fusz, who supported secession and saw no evil in slavery, encountered Union General William Rosecrans, who had assumed
command of the Department of Missouri on January 30. After seeing
Rosecrans, Fusz pondered in his journal about the piety and sincerity of
the general. He seemed unable to think that Rosecrans could truly share
his religious beliefs.

The chance encounter was at Annunciation Church, then facing Sixth
Street south of Chouteau, near Busch Stadium. Fusz's journal entries also
reflect on the predicament of denominations and churches during a civil
war.

Sunday April 10th, 1864

I was awakened this morning at an early hour, by Mother, to
rise and attend mass with the St. Vincent de Paul Society at the
Annunciation Church. How soft and sweet the bed seemed when
I had to leave it. Heavy clouds hung in heaven and uncertain
weather seemed to be in for the day. I walked to church. There
were about 200 members of the Society present. I here saw for
the first time "Rosecranz" the Command of this department. He
approached a pew in front of mine, but being locked, he could not
enter; he then went around to a side aisle and reverently heard
mass and approached Holy Communion with the members. His
whole demeanor was attentive, retired and pious. Can his acts in
religion here be sincere or is it policy that moves him, that he makes
himself prominent at all Catholic festivals and celebrations and by

public acts of piety calls forth the notice of his piety? From his appearance I judge him to be sincere, even to fanaticism in his faith and his political opinion, yet it is a question whether he does not try to use one for the advancement of the other and vice-versa as the case may be. I can in this instance, only testify that his conduct was most unassuming and becoming a Christian.

From his portraits, I had imagined him to be dark haired and whiskered, hence but for his strongly marked features and prominent nose would not have known him. When I first noticed him, I saw a fair haired and rudy cheeked gentleman of good mien and thought him an unknown member of one of the lower conferences. Something military in his dress changed my idea and a close scrutiny revealed the true character of the visitor.

I took breakfast with my friends Joseph Imbe and Moriarty. In the Republican newspaper of today I noticed a long report of the proceedings of the Presbyterian Synod in regard to membership with such as had been or were rebels. While regretting that politics had come into their church, these representatives did their best to increase the bitter feelings therein. This rebellion had before by them been declared a sin and its adherents sinners. Of course under our military regime, this is an easy declaration, but the case would have been very different had the Southern cause triumphed and its arms held sway here. Here is a private interpretation allowed to members (according to the Protestant dogma) and yet an express declaration of sin. Some remarkable acknowledgements were made in the debate, the most important being the avowal of the numbers that have in consequence of these troubles joined the Catholic church and the general preference expressed for the same, because she has kept aloof from politics, achieving the idea that the sermons and teachings must be of a political nature, instead of the word of God. No wonder men's minds are opened to this fact.

Later in the same entry, he described the cornerstone laying for the original St. Anthony of Padua Church on Meramec Street. The area's German residents had attended Mass said in a community room in the nearby House of Refuge. After that orphanage was transformed into a Union hospital, the German settlers founded St. Anthony Parish.

This afternoon my friends named above and myself went to assist at the laying of the corner stone of a new church in the southern suburbs of town to be named after St. Antonio of Padua, for the Franciscan fathers. The concourses of people was immense. A Catholic's heart was gladdened at beholding twice 17 or 18 cars on the R.R. track, overcrowded inside and outside with eager witnesses whose substantial offerings would swell the sum with which to pay the building expenses . . .

Fusz Diary, Vol. II, 28–29.

JULIA DENT GRANT

Julia Dent Grant returned to White Haven during the winter of 1864 to care for their son Fred who was very ill. While there, a Confederate acquaintance paid a visit. She identified the acquaintance only as Mary. She may have been Mary Bowen, wife of the late General John Bowen who had helped defend Vicksburg against Grant's siege.

While in St. Louis, an old acquaintance called to see the General to get a pass through the lines so she could join her husband's friends in Georgia. Poor thing! She had lost her husband at Vicksburg, fighting on the Confederate side. I was very sorry for her, and, although she had not asked for me, I told the servant when she called again I wished to see her. When she came, I went down, taking with me a roll of Confederate bills captured at Vicksburg and given me as a souvenir, amounting to something over $4,000 and, handing her the permit wrapped around these bills, I said: "Dear Mary, I hope the enclosure may be of use to you. They were given me simply as souvenirs." My conscience troubled me after she left. I feared I had aided the cause of secession and confessed the whole to my husband, who only smiled at my fears and said I had done a service to the Union in doing just as I had; that the more of that kind of money there was in circulation, the better it would be for us.

That spring, Julia and her family participated in the giant fair that was a fund-raiser for the Western Sanitary Commission.

The children were much excited with their attendance at the great Sanitary Fair, which had just been held at St. Louis. Nellie had been representing the old woman in the shoe who had so many children she didn't know what to do. Nellie was delighted with her metamorphosis, seated as she was in a mammoth black pasteboard shoe filled with beautiful dolls of all sizes. Nellie wore over her pretty curls a wide, ruffled cap and a pair of huge spectacles across her pretty, rosy, dimpled face. She was delighted with the selling of dolls and her photos, telling me the ladies gave her a half dollar for every doll and every picture. She gave one of these to me with much pride. My darling boys, too, filled my lap with all the pretty things they had secured by purchase and raffle on this occasion, some of which I have yet.

Julia Dent Grant, 126, 131.

GALUSHA ANDERSON

As the war wore on and the demands on charities continued to grow, the Western Sanitary Commission looked to other cities for fund-raising ideas. The sanitary commissions in eastern cities and Chicago had bolstered their shrinking funds by holding fairs.

Inspired by their fairs, the Western Sanitary Commission opened a huge fair in St. Louis on May 17, 1864. The fair building constructed on 12th Street (Tucker Boulevard) from Olive to St. Charles streets was 500 feet long and 114 feet wide. The wings on Locust Street stretched 100 feet each and were 54 feet wide.

A fine arts exhibit, floral park, displays of agricultural equipment and sewing machines, gold and silver bars from Nevada, and an exhibition of war trophies filled the building. Handmade and manufactured articles had been donated by St. Louisans and supporters from throughout the Union and from England and Germany.

The fair netted over half a million dollars.

In his memoir of the war years, Galusha Anderson described some of the diplomatic delicacies demanded to organize a fund-raiser that involved both beer-drinking Germans and temperance people.

The Germans, being so large a part of our population, and so ardently devoted to the maintenance of the Union, were given a large space in the building, where they patriotically sold lager beer, and a host of people patriotically drank it. Very many connected with the Fair strongly objected to this, but being in the minority were unable to prevent it.

During the days of preparation for the Fair a committee was appointed to meet a delegation from our German fellow-citizens and if possible persuade them to give up the project of selling beer at the Fair. I was chairman, and presented as well as I could the earnest desire of the temperance people. The German, who was the spokesman of his delegation, understood English quite perfectly, but could not speak it very well. He had not been at all persuaded by the considerations that I had presented, and among other things that he vehemently urged in reply was this: "Zhentelmen," said he, "lager peer vill not make men trunk; it vill not, it vill not. Zhentelmen, and ef any one gets trunk, we have already, zhentelmen, engaged the police to take him to de calaboose." So this, and every effort that we put forth to rid the Fair of lager beer, proved abortive; and it was sold, innumerable kegs of it, to alleviate the sufferings of our soldiers. But in justice it ought to be added that no one became so intoxicated that it was necessary to take him to the calaboose.

Anderson described scenes at the Sanitary Fair that reflected the changing social order in St. Louis.

The evenings at the Fair were made specially attractive. Then the men that had been absorbed in business during the day came with their families. The great building was lighted as brilliantly as it could be with gas. . . . In the gallery trained bands skillfully discoursed patriotic music. Often the commanding general with his staff, in their brightest uniform, was present. It is wonderful how the crowd is charmed by military clothes! The names of the Union generals together with the names of the battles that they had fought were blazoned on the walls, and the Stars and Stripes hung out everywhere, while women from the first families of the city were busy selling all sorts of useful articles. No one who shared in those festivities, who saw and heard and drank in the spirit of that patriotic throng can ever forget it.

One feature was specially novel. The colored soldiers, enlisted and drilled under the direction of General Schofield, during the Fair constantly did guard duty. They also distinguished themselves, and greatly commended themselves to all right-minded people, by liberally contributing from their meagre wages to aid the refugees and freedmen. Colored people also freely visited the Fair and made purchases. It looked like a revolution when we saw, in a slave State, white women of high social standing, without complaint or a murmur, sell articles to colored purchasers. Once or twice indeed some whites took offence at this radical and apparently abrupt change from the old order of things, but on the whole the sentiment toward the colored people was humane, reasonable, and liberal.

The Fair proved a great financial success. Its net proceeds were five hundred and fifty-four thousand five hundred and ninety-one dollars, at least three dollars and fifty cents for each inhabitant of our city; but the result was largely due to contributors beyond our borders; nevertheless it can be said of St. Louis that she did the work which made this great success possible, and at the same time liberally gave to the Fair both merchandise and money. The large amount of money realized, together with other donations, enabled the Sanitary Commission to complete its great work. In addition to the sums of money that it directly disbursed to aid our armies, it appropriated to the Ladies' Union Aid Society fifty thousand dollars for hospital work and the assistance of soldiers' families. It also devoted one thousand dollars per month to the aid of the freedmen, and established at Webster, ten miles west of the city, a Soldiers' Orphans' Home, at a cost from first to last of over forty thousand dollars. The Home accommodated one hundred and fifty fatherless children.

But the Fair was a blessing not only to refugees and freedmen, to the sick and wounded in hospitals, to the widows and orphans of our slain heroes, but it was also a measureless boon to St. Louis. It was one more mighty agency for curing us of our selfishness. For a time at least it broke in upon our commercialism, and led us to think of others and to do something for their welfare.

Galusha Anderson, 311–14.

HUGH CAMPBELL

Brother and partner of St. Louis businessman Robert Campbell, Hugh Campbell wrote to their nephew John Hamilton, on May 19, 1864. After expressing relief that Hamilton was not seriously wounded, Hugh succinctly described the challenges the Civil War posed to St. Louis commerce. He also noted that Chicago's commerce benefited from St. Louis's woe. This loss to St. Louis business would persist after the war.

Dear John. Your letter of 2nd ult reached us [after much detention] some days ago. We had previously known that you were wounded, and now feel greatly relieved to learn from yourself that the wound was not so serious as we had apprehended. It is hoped that when this reaches you your wound & general health will be restored. We rejoice to learn that your wife is with you. With such nursing & society you have important aids to your Surgeon. One letter

Hugh Campbell, courtesy Campbell House Museum

only has been received from you since this sad war began and that was written probably at the suggestion of Gen Hallack. You were doubtless too busy in the discharge of your military duties—but surely you might have spared enough time to tell us something about yourself. The newspapers tell us enough about other things. Business in St. Louis has been prostrate for nearly three years owing chiefly to Military and Treasury restriction on trading. Lately it has revived a little yet a long time must elapse before it is restored to its former prosperity. Chicago businessmen have fattened on our leanness and time alone can bring back prosperity to St. Louis. Robert has three children left out of thirteen. Hugh is now 16—a fine boy, over 6 ft high. He is a student at Washington College and has made fair progress in his studies. Hazlett is over six, and Jimmie [Jas about over four]. They are all great sources of comfort and pleasure to their old uncle. Our wives are well—and so are all our connection here. We reside near to each other, and both families are like one. At each house there is a mother-in-law and sister-in-law. All seems to be attached to each other—and it appears like one family occupying two houses. In these sad times we have sources of pleasure, within our circle. . . . Gen Hunter dined with us two months ago. I told him that you were our nephew but forbore to ask questions. He made no other remarks than that you were chief of Artillery. As I am not an admirer of the fanatical Gen. I was grateful that he said nothing about you. It infer that you are not a fanatic It will give us all great pleasure to hear from you soon. You do not say which arm was wounded. We presume from your excellent handwriting, that it must be the left arm. All of our household desire to be remembered to you & to Mrs. Hamilton Yours Sincerely-

Hugh Campbell

Robert Campbell Papers, Campbell House Museum.

LOUIS PHILIP FUSZ

The journal entries of Louis Fusz are filled with observations on the arrests of local Southern sympathizers, reactions to war news, and fear of the military drafts. This Confederate wrote with a mix of hope and glee at every hardship and misfortune the Union faced. He found Union policies and Lincoln's actions tyrannical. Until the presidential election of 1864, he was confident that the Union would fail.

The following journal excerpts from the spring and summer of 1864, show no awareness of how devastating the Union victories the previous summer at Vicksburg and Gettysburg had been to the Confederacy.

Grant and Lee were battling in the Wilderness while Fusz wrote in his journal on Sunday May 8, 1864, about the failings of the Union and about more local arrests of suspected Southern spies.

Sunday May 8th, 1864

These arrests however have not the same affect they used to have at first. They are taken more as a matter of course of no great consequence and do not carry the dread and terror which they did at first. The fact is that tyranny is felt to be more despicable and that its reign is near its end. I have a strong conviction that this is the last year of the war. A general weariness is experienced, its results are to say the least doubtful and the ruin already incurred so great that a further continuance is not relished. If Grant fails, the end is near.

On Thursday, August 4, Fusz described the hard times that he hoped would lead to the fall of the Union.

Yet while all the people are intent on amusements, dire calamities remain suspended above their heads; not to speak of the conscription of 500,000 men ordered of the 5 of September; the crisis is the war seems near at hand. Already there are signs of distress among the people. Food high, clothing enormous, taxes awful, and it is difficult for the mass to make a fair living. The demand for labor is slackening and though thus far wages have been high too, yet there is a disposition, owing to the slackening of trade and industry, to lower them . . .

Later, in the same entry and again on September 4 and on September 18, he discussed the upcoming presidential election. He wrote almost dismissively of Lincoln, made a case for his defeat in his bid for reelection, and believed that a President George McClellan would sue for peace.

Here is the Presidential election approaching and the jocular occupant of the office, presents his claims for a reelection. Hundreds of thousands of lives lost, thousands of millions spent, the country desolated, homes broken up and the whole nation nearly bankrupt, such are these claims. On the moral side I was going to name the debasement of the people, their loss of the spirit of freedom, their baseness, but one thought convinces me that with the mass of Americans, he is not the cause; that they themselves were in that condition for a long time past and that all their blustering and bragging about their freedom, their self respect, etc. were only loud proclamations to things that they felt they possessed no more. Hence, on what other grounds account for the rapidity of the visible debasement, for the immediate yielding to quasi absolute power.

September 4, 1864

The Democratic nomination for candidates at the next presidential election are made and are a terror to the opponents. McClellan for President, Pendleton for Vice President, a peace Platform such are the men and the measures bro't before the people in November next and their success if undisturbed by military power is very hopeful. Peace is undoubtedly the wish of the whole Democratic party; rather with the Union restored if possible, but peace anyhow at last. T'is well to come to senses again, though it were far better had sense been used from the first and thousands upon thousands of lives been spared and untold wealth saved.

Sunday Sept. 18th 1864

The Democratic Convention was held Monday, Sept. 5th, and strong peace feelings were exhibited. To the dismay of its enemies, its sitting was harmonious and they nominated Genl. McClellan their candidate for the Presidency. George H. Pendleton of Ohio, a thorough Peace man, was elected Vice President. The choice of McClellan was because of his availability as he more than any other man could balance the army vote. He belongs to the faction called War Democracy, yet his sentiments are for a fair settlement of our difficulties. He states to Mr. Harrison who saw him about that time that he would offer an armistice and call for a convention of States, showing a willingness to take the first steps for the reestablishment of peace . . .

On Sunday, September 25, Fusz wrote about the draft being conducted throughout the city, ward by ward. (Fusz lived with his parents on North Seventh Street, just north of downtown, in the Ninth Ward.) He hinted that if drafted he might flee to join the Confederate Army.

There was a Dft. on the 19th, beginning with the first district, of which the 4th ward of this city is the first sub-division. It was a rough thing; almost every man drawn. The 5th ward also was drafted from. The whole created a tremendous consternation among all men affected, such a general stampede, I never beheld. On Friday the Dft. was stopped to enable the authorities to notify the individuals already drawn; also to examine them and to receive their substitutes. At the rate of proceeding, it will be two weeks before they reach the 9th ward, in which Eugene and myself are enrolled. Many have already left that are enrolled in it. I pray that the Dft. may be spun out in length, until the Presidential election so that an individual may act with discernment. In fact, if Lincoln is reelected, it is war, war, desolation, ruin. With McClellan there are still some hopes.

In consequence of the great demand and the fears of the drafted men, substitutes have commanded an extreme price. As much as $1500 has been paid for one. At present the excitement has somewhat subsided and the price ranges as low as $500 to 550 to serve for one year . . .

The tone and attitudes in Fusz's journal began to change in September of 1864, after his younger brother Paul was arrested while sneaking out of St. Louis to join the Confederacy. In the entries on September 25 and 26, Fusz relates how he learned that Paul, who was at odds with their family, attempted to join the Confederate armies, but was captured. Since he was wearing part of a Union uniform, he was imprisoned as a spy. Paul worked with Louis at the firm of Chouteau, Harrison and Valle.

[Paul] came to the office as usual but did not speak to me.

In the afternoon of next day, Thursday, he was absent and not returning on Friday, we made inquiries and all information proved that he had left. So Paul is gone, gone to the Southern armies, to privation, to sufferings, and perhaps to death! . . .

Monday 26th Sept. 1864
Mr. Dugan came into our office this morning and calling me aside told me that he had just seen Paul marching down street under guard as a prisoner. He had a long grey coat on and it was reported half a Federal Lieutenant's suit. More he could not tell. His dream of glory is then at an end, for the present at least. He has then been captured . . .

On Sunday 30th, October, 1864,

The past week has been an important one to me. The Draft had at last reached our 9th ward and I am happy to say that with God's grace both Eugene and myself escaped being drawn. Three hundred names were drawn each day to the last and forteen hundred and twenty-two in all came from the dreaded box. Impatience was felt as soon as the hour of 3 came nigh and a close watch set for a newspaper boy with the evening 2nd edition. Once obtained, carefully and one by one the last was scrutinized and at the end a pause and the utterance, was "thank God", three hundred better. Each evening Eugene would run home to carry the tidings, also would stop at friends houses similarly situated. But amidst the rejoicing I cannot but feel that this is only a respite. I now expect to remain home over winter, but next spring? . . .

On Monday morning November 14, Fusz reacted to Lincoln's re-election and, resentful, dreamt of emigrating to Mexico.

This country's fate for the next 4 years and perhaps for much longer is foreshadowed by the result of the presidential elections on the 8th inst. Lincoln is reelected by an astonishing majority. Hoping against hope, it was thought by us that yet McClellan might be the successful candidate. Fearful of foul play on the part of the administration, we had watched and thought to the last moment that all was fair and on the eventful day slept in fancyful security to be awakened next morning by most gloomy news.

Strange to say, the election in its results seemed to have been the expression of the people. New York where they had also a governor's election, seems to have cast her choice also for Lincoln and exchanged the man who has kept up her States dignity for one who is the tool of the central power . . .

The above result brings now more forcibly the idea of a [new] course of life. As I feared before, and more so now, the prospects of this country are painful indeed. National prosperity will not be recovered; speculators, "shoddyites" and other rascals may fill their pockets, but at the expense of the people. Political differences of opinion will hardly be tolerated; more than ever, moderation will be insulted and retirement threatened. Conscription with renewed vigor will be carried out and thus happy prospects blotted out. The question is again agitated of abandoning all here and joining the army. I am fully impressed that it is not a life of pleasures and even of glory alone. I know that privations, sufferings are the rule and plenty and ease the exception; yet I can stand what others can. But mother is utterly opposed to the purpose and under the present painful circumstances attending my bro. Paul's imprisonment, I feel hardly justified in adding to her cup of sorrow.

I am almost ashamed to acknowledge it. But devotion to a cause, thirst for glory, for fame, has almost given place this past week to the idea of emigration. Wealth and affluences have now presented themselves in the most inviting colors. Mexico who seems now to have become pacified, is the smiling field. Visions of plantations, or of mines, in which industry is exercised and rewarded stand before my eyes. Joe Imbs, for sometime past, has entertained views on that country and expressed them warmly, but without presenting them in a concise practical form and the last to me is the most important, . . . He urges emigration there very pressingly but I gave it very little heed. Two or three days ago an old farmer from Howard Co., an acquaintance of Mr. Harrison called in and bluntly asked the latter where to go. "To Mexico of course. Maximilian's empire bids fair to be stable and prosperity will follow. Or you might go to Brazil which I like best, because slavery exists there. But still Mexico is very promising and another thing that you will approve of is the debarring of emigration by Yankees bringing Puritan principles . . ."

After further pondering of Mexico, and the best ways for a group of expatriates to travel there, he commented on his brother Paul's circumstances.

[Paul] is still in Gratiot Street Prison. Always rash. . . . The reports from him continue good, the turnkeys etc. seem to esteem him for his manliness and willingness, but still his letters, specially his secret letters, breathe the wretchedness of his condition. Poor food and scanty at that. Last Monday, I paid a visit, introduced by Father Roe, to the Pro. Mar. [Provost Marshal] Col. Darr, and tried to obtain the permission of sending him food at times; also that his chains should be removed from his leg. I was refused, though politely treated. He is a hard hearted man, who thinks it his duty to be severe as possible to his prisoners . . .

Louis Philip Fusz Diary, Vol. II, 35, 50, 58-62; Vol. III, 9, 14-17.

1865

"sorrow and tears trod on the heels of joy"
—*Galusha Anderson on the assassination of Lincoln*

The inevitable end of the war was nearing, and it was nearly impossible to deny even for the most rabid secessionists. While Grant forced Lee to stretch his withered army along longer and longer defenses around Petersburg, Sherman turned north from conquered Charleston, South Carolina. Through woods and through swamps, his army built their own roads as they marched north. They averaged ten miles a day through the Carolinas and marching toward Grant's forces.

In Missouri, Radical Republicans, who supported immediate emancipation, had swept most of the races in the 1864 elections. Since the Emancipation Proclamation had not applied to Missouri, a slave state, the State Legislature authorized a constitutional convention to consider emancipation. The convention opened in the Old Courthouse in Downtown St. Louis on January 7, 1865. Four days later, to loud applause, the delegates overwhelmingly approved the ordinance for unconditional freedom to Missouri slaves.

Meanwhile, Lincoln maneuvered the Thirteenth Amendment, abolishing slavery, through Congress on January 31.

The Western Sanitary Commission converted the old Lawson Hospital on Broadway for a refugee and freedmen's home able to accommodate six hundred persons. From February 1 to July 10, 1865, the institution provided shelter, food, medical care, and schooling to several thousand refugees, freed people, and their children.

On March 4, Abraham Lincoln was inaugurated for his second term. His assassination would ensure that his inauguration speech, pleaing for malice toward none, would fall on deaf ears.

Nathan D. Allen, a New York native who settled in St. Louis in 1837, kept a journal with succinct entries. A bookkeeper at Mechanics Bank, he lived on Compton Avenue. His journal entries were chilling—headlines of momentous news and of the mood in St. Louis during the spring and summer of 1865. The entries succinctly sum up the year 1865.

April 1	*Peach trees in bloom in St. Louis*
April 3	*Richmond and Petersburg evacuated*
April 9	*Lees Army surrender at Appomattox*
April 14	*President Lincoln Assassinated at 9:30 p.m.*
April 15	*President died at 7:30 a.m. The day was to have been a day of jubilee. But was turned into Mourning, Mobile surrendered.*
April 16	*(Allen described the sentiment in St. Louis) Sunday Churches crowded universal feeling of sorrow and horror and determination that no mercy shall be shown to rebels until the last end of rebelion and slavery*
April 19	*Funeral at Washington*
April 20	*Johnson surrendered to Sherman.*
April 26	*Booth the Assassin killed.*
April 27	*Steamer Sultana blown up 1500 lives lost.*

During the month of May, Allen made only two, but profound, entries. He noted "Jefferson Davis captured" on May 10, and on May 26 he wrote, "Genl Kirby surrendered the last of the Rebel Army."

As men were returning home from war, and beds in the local hospitals started to stay empty, Allen only made one entry in his diary during the entire month of July. "July 7 The Asassins hung—"

On August 31, his simple entry reflected his own—and the whole city's—transition from the war back to peacetime interests: "The past month has been cool and pleasant like September."

JOHN BATES JOHNSON

J ohn Bates Johnson, physician and leader of the Western Sanitary Commission, wrote to his brother Henry on January 15, 1865. After apologies for not writing family members more often, he then celebrated the news of Missouri abolishing slavery.

I feel very sure that you will rejoice with us today in giving thanks to Almighty God for His wonderful dealings with us in making Missouri a <u>Free State</u>. The ordinance was passed on the 11th instant at 3:00 p.m. by a vote of 61 to 4, declaring that from the passage of this ordinance, slavery forever ceased in Missouri. Since then we have had nothing but salutes, bonfires, illuminations and huzzas. The negroes are about the happiest mortals I have seen. They all seem calm, not disposed to any outbreak as evidence of their joy, but their faces seem lit up with new hope that they are free. Today in most of our churches we had thanksgiving to God for His goodness and mercy unto us. Sermons have been preached appropriate to so glorious an event, and, from this time forth, the 11th of January will be celebrated by us, our children and our children's children, to the remotest time as the day of our escape from bondage—the bondage from slavery—and as the day which ushered in the full enjoyment of civil and religious freedom to all the inhabitants of the State of Missouri. When I came to Missouri I thought it would eventually be a free State, not in my day, but in the life-time perhaps of some of my children. God has most signally shown His Power by changing the hearts of men and bringing this result about at a time and in a way we know not of. To Him be all the glory.

Johnson Papers, Missouri History Museum Archives.

LILLIE BALMER UNGER

illie Balmer Unger was the daughter of the noted violinist, composer, and owner of a music store, Charles Balmer. A German immigrant who had settled in St. Louis in 1839, Charles Balmer fostered the music industry in the upstart river town. He lived on the south side of Papin Street between Fifteenth and Sixteenth streets.

Lillie's handwritten reminiscences in a notebook contain this memory from the last year of the war. Her father inadvertently had displayed sheet music for a Confederate march in his shop window on Fourth Street near the Old Courthouse.

In 1865, one side of 14th & Papin was called the Union Row & across the street the Secess. Father put the wrong march in his show case & landed in McDowell's College an army jail on 8th & Gratiot—mother made herring & potato salad & Sauer Braten with bottles of wine treated the officers at the jail & brought Dad home. Mother was a pretty woman of great charm & winning ways. Father was wealthy & our cellar contained wines, beer & champagne—our parlors were crowded every Sun. Mother entertained with charades & she had 2 long tables in the attic, full of costumes: maid & coachman—Frank-Henry Mohrman of St. Charles—took wheels off of surrey barouche—put runners on & had a sleigh, with buffalo robes.

Lillie Balmer Unger Notebook, 9, Missouri History Museum Archives.

Louis Philip Fusz

L ouis Fusz did not follow his dreams of leaving for Mexico but sought freedom for his imprisoned brother Paul, who had been transferred to the penitentiary in Jefferson City. On Friday, March 3, he received word that President Lincoln had pardoned Paul.

As Louis traveled by train to Jefferson City to deliver the good news, he noted the signs of General Sterling Price's invasion of Missouri the previous fall.

I felt also interested as we sped along in watching the trace of the recent rebel raid which could plainly be detected along the Road in remnants of burnt cars etc. and which would also be suggested by the sight of the new water tanks and new bridges rebuilt in lieu of the old ones destroyed.

Though Lincoln had pardoned his brother, Fusz still did not admire the president, his skills as a leader, nor his eloquence. He ridiculed Lincoln's second inaugural address, which is recognized as one of the great speeches of American history.

On the 4th inst. the reinauguaration of Pres. Lincoln took place. A speech delivered by him on the occasion may be said merely to prove his acquaintance with the phrascology of the old testament without whedding new light on the state of the country or giving hopes for the future. He acknowledges that by this war the nation is doing penance for its past sins, namely that of slavery; admits that the strife was not exactly begun by the South and also that it may yet continue an indefinite length of time. Its chief, if not only merit, is its brevity: 2 minutes reading will go over it.

His journal entry made on Easter Monday, April 17, 1865, indicates that the news of Lincoln's assassination shocked Fusz. Suddenly, Fusz understood Lincoln's importance to the entire nation.

Good God! What a shock to the country! It could not be true! It is a joke . . . and yet t'is no joke but sad reality. President Lincoln has been assassinated! . . .

For once in the annals of this country's history, its chief falls by the hands of the assassin. Now, when more than ever his presence is necessary; when his known lenient disposition is needed to guide the political affairs to a peaceful haven, he is no more; . . .

Fusz Diary, Vol. III, 60, 66-67, 69.

GALUSHA ANDERSON

A s pastor of the Second Baptist Church of St. Louis at the corner of Sixth and Locust streets, Galusha Anderson had a window on the character, mood, and politics of St. Louis. In his memoir of the Civil War, he described the jubilant atmosphere on the city streets after news spread of the surrender of General Lee and the Army of Northern Virginia.

That 10th of April was memorable not only for the whole nation, but also especially for St. Louis. A border city, which, for four long years, had been a bone of contention, fought over and snarled over by the dogs of war, had perhaps a keener appreciation of the surrender of the illustrious Lee, than could be found in any city far to the north of Mason and Dixon's line. At all events no pen however able and eloquent could adequately depict our joy on the day which followed Grant's final victory in Virginia. No business was done, except that which was most necessary and perfunctory. Men spontaneously gathered in crowds, their faces radiant, their lips rippling with smiles; they shook hands with firm grip; with tears starting in their eyes they talked of the surrender; all bitterness seemed to be gone; there was little or no exultation over those who had laid down their arms; men on every hand just brimmed over with gladness that the fratricidal strife had ended, and that slavery, the fruitful cause of our greatest woes, was no more.

And it was remarkable how few secessionists there were in our city on that day. During the four preceding years they had been alarmingly numerous, but now only a very few could be found; they had been strangely and magically transformed into Unionists.

Even those who for four years had sat on the fence hopped off on the Union side, flapped their wings and crowed.

Still our city was not a unit in political thought and sentiment. While Grant's victory caused the great multitude to rejoice, it was wormwood and gall to the few, who, in spite of disaster to the Confederacy, were still faithful to it. While their neighbors were exultant, they bitterly mourned. The city put on its gala dress. Public buildings and private dwellings were lavishly decorated with red, white and blue. National flags of all sizes were flung to the breeze. But here and there a house was flagless. Within sat sad and sombre secessionists sighing over their shattered hopes. They refused to be comforted. At night once more the bells rang, bands played, bonfires blazed, cannon boomed, and the windows of most buildings, public and private, were illuminated; while in public halls the people gathered to listen to patriotic speeches and to sing the most popular and stirring war songs. "The Star Spangled Banner," "Rally Round the Flag, Boys," and "The Soul of Old John Brown," had a large place in our festivity, while "My Country, 'Tis of Thee," was sung as the crowning and parting hymn."

After describing the joyous celebrations, Anderson wrote of the devastating news of Lincoln's assassination. He described an incident that reflected the explosive anger in St. Louis.

But sorrow and tears trod on the heels of joy. April 15th, five days after our exultant celebration of Lee's surrender, came the astounding news that our great President had been shot the night before at Ford's Theatre, in Washington, and that he had died in the morning. For an hour or two we were dazed by this sudden and overwhelming calamity. No one thought of doing business. Those who gathered on the Board of Trade did nothing but talk over the crushing national sorrow. Men as if in a dream moved along the streets; few said anything; they dumbly shook hands and passed sadly on; as the most stalwart met, tears started; the city was silent and a pall of gloom rested upon all. Men at last began slowly to drift together in companies upon the streets. They conversed in low but earnest tones. Beneath that calm exterior fierce passion burned.

On Fourth Street a great, excited crowd had instinctively gathered; they, like all others, were talking over the appalling national loss. A stranger passed by. They thought that he expressed himself as pleased with the assassination of Mr. Lincoln. In a moment the pent up fires within them flashed forth. They seized the stranger, beat him, dragged him roughly along the pavement, he all the time pleading to be heard. At last they listened to his statement and were convinced that they had quite misunderstood what they believed to have been a grossly offensive utterance. They were deeply ashamed of what they had passionately done, and humbly apologized for it. But the incident showed that life of any one in our city, who, on that day, should have openly approved of the murder of the President, would have been indignantly snuffed out.

Anderson described the appearance of a city draped in mourning.

Throughout the city all flags were at half-mast. On public buildings, churches and private dwellings, the emblems of rejoicing gave place to those of mourning. Public sentiment was such that no one living in the better part of the residential districts dared to withhold the ordinary tokens of the general sorrow. Houses that five days before were conspicuously dark amid the almost universal illumination were now draped in black; some it may be in self-defence, but probably in most cases as the expression of genuine sorrow. . . . The same lips that four years before had scornfully called him clown, the Illinois ape, baboon and gorilla, now praised him. He had not only subdued the rebellion by force of arms, but also by his clearness of conception, fairness in administration, unflinching advocacy of the rights of all, patience and persistence in duty, and large-heartedness, had conquered their inveterate prejudices.

In the afternoon of that day of sorrow, the churches were thrown open, and large congregations met to pray. They poured out their hearts in thanksgiving to God for the unsullied life of the martyred President; for his courage and wisdom in proclaiming liberty to the captive, and freedom to the oppressed. They prayed for his constitutional successor in office, and for God's blessing on the people both North and South. . . . At last the curtain of darkness fell on that terrible day, and men with throbbing brows and aching hearts lay down to rest; but to many, if sleep came at all, it came but fitfully. We seemed to be living in a new world. One era of our national life had ended, another had begun. . . .

Anderson, 361–64.

THE REVEREND
SAMUEL J. NICCOLLS

O n April 23, 1865, only nine days after the assassination, the Reverend Samuel J. Niccolls delivered "A Discourse on the Assassination of Abraham Lincoln," at the Second Presbyterian Church. The church was located at Fifth and Walnut streets (just south of the present-day Ballpark Hilton).

Twenty-six-year-old Niccolls had been a chaplain of a Pennsylvania regiment from Antietam to Fredericksburg. He had joined his new congregation only a few months earlier. During the next fifty years, he averaged a sermon a day and became popularly known as "the Presbyterian bishop of the West."

He described Lincoln in biblical terms. Lincoln had been jeered as a buffoon, had mastered political division with wit and humor, and had been tortured by the challenges of leading the Union Cause. His assassination had instantly shed a new light, that normally can only come with time, on the late president. Niccolls' sixteen-page discourse reflected how the assassination quickly transformed the understanding of President Abraham Lincoln.

Undoubtedly, many local Confederate sympathizers took pleasure from the assassination, even quietly rejoicing. However, it was the voice of the grieving that was heard in the halls, on the street corner, and echoed through the churches.

Niccolls began his discourse by expounding on a passage from the Bible, which led into these comments.

Lately there has come to us the report of a deed so dark and damning in its character, that one might well be excused for thinking it too horrible to be true. It fell upon us in the midst of our joy, like a clap of thunder from a serene and sunlit sky. We were as one staggered by a sudden blow, and went to our homes that woeful day, struck dumb with horror and amazement. And well might it be so, for when Abraham Lincoln fell bleeding from that vile murderer's weapon, a deed was committed, which for infamy and atrocity, stands without a parallel in our history. Not in the records of modern times, but in the bloody annals of barbarous days, when poison and the assasin's knife were the favorite instruments of tyrants and traitors, must we look to find a crime which does not seem like a virtue, when compared with this unnatural murder. We are humiliated when we hear the dreadful story repeated; for mingled with sorrow for the dead, and indignation against the perpetrators of the act, there is a sense of shame oppressing every true heart, that such a deed should stain our country's history. We feel as some proud father, when he learns that a vile adulterer has robbed him of his honor, by blackening with crime the escutcheon of his family's purity, handed down to him unsullied through a long line of noble ancestors. If the tears of a bereaved nation, if the blood of the wretched murderer, and the fears of his guilty accomplices in treason, could purge from our history this dark sin, it were soon done. But it admits of no atonement, no palliation. It is one of these great crimes, that stop the pleading of mercy, and cry with the voice of martyred blood for vengeance.

Later in the sermon, Niccolls remarked on the character of the late president.

[Lincoln's] generous heart could harbor no resentment, and cherish no sentiments of revenge. It pleased him better to pardon than to punish, and to overcome his and the country's enemies by transforming them into friends. Alas! that so gentle a heart must be

driven from earth by the hand of murder. His intellectual quali-
ties, though not of the highest order of genius, were such as, beyond all question, gave him a peculiar capacity for the duties of
his office. Quick in his perceptions, and of a keen logical mind, his
good sense, conjoined with his sterling integrity, served him better
in extremity than diplomacy. His knowledge of human nature was
profound, and it was from men and their actions more than from
any theory of law or ethics, that he drew his arguments and illus-
trations of policy. I do not forget, while commending his virtues,
that he had enemies who bitterly denounced him, for his life was
no exception to the great law that those who stand for righteous-
ness and truth, must "suffer persecution", and be reviled falsely.
Strange would it have been, in war with Slavery, if the author of
the Emancipation Proclamation, and the great representative of
Freedom, had been treated otherwise. It has been charged against
him as the most culpable of his faults, that he was light and frivo-
lous at times. . . .

Such are some of the characteristics of the man who, until a
few days ago, sat in the seat of Washington, the honored head of a
mighty republic. He was not perfect, but great and good in face of
his imperfections. Yet, looking at his character in the transforming
light of death, which so strangely turns the blemishes into shad-
ows, and thus brings out more perfectly the beauties of the life picture, it is difficult to see what we could alter without also affecting
the perfection of his work for this people. Called to preside over the
destinies of the nation in the most stormy and eventful period of
its life, he stood faithfully and conscientiously at his post, and at last
saw his policy not only endorsed by the people in his re-election,
but vindicated by success. Like Moses of old, he had led the people
through the wilderness of trial, and already saw with glad eyes the
green hill tops and smiling valleys of the land of peace and rest.
With thoughts of mercy, and intent on peace, he was preparing to
lead us to its full fruition, when suddenly, like the breath of frost to
the blossoms of spring, there came these tidings to pall our hopes

and turn universal joy into mourning—*he is dying*. Did we not all see the dreadful sight,—the bed of death with its stifled grief, the noble form motionless, save that its breast heaved to the laboring breath—grave senators with faces bathed in tears—sobs that come from the adjoining room—the noiseless attendants—the anxious surgeons watching the tremor of the waning pulse? And soon, like a knell heard throughout the wide land, went the message, *he is dead*. Yes, dead! my countrymen. Foully murdered by the hand of treason! "Help, Lord, for the godly man ceaseth; for the faithful fail among the children of men." Oh! day of horror and awful judgment! when, in an instant, the bright sky of our joy is hung with clouds of woe. From border to border and sea to sea, the land mourns. It is as if a corpse lay in every homestead. Business is suspended. Grief makes every true heart throb heavily. Men grasp each other by the hand, made brothers in sorrow, and heart speaks its sympathy to heart in expressive silence, or through falling tears. Such was the man, and such his throne in the hearts of the people, whom murder and treason, "Two yoke devils sworn to either's purpose," singled out among others as the first victim for the assassin's blow.

Niccolls concluded his sixteen-page sermon with this thought.

. . . we will rejoice; for in that day, my countrymen, whose dawning we may now see, this glorious banner, no longer draped in mourning, but flung to the breeze, and purified from every stain of dishonor, shall be the true emblem of gospel liberty, and the symbol of the freest, strongest, and most Christian nation on the face of the earth.

Rev. Samuel J. Niccolls, A Discourse on the Assassination of Abraham Lincoln *(St. Louis: Sherman Spencer, Printer, 1865), 3, 7-9, 16. St. Louis Public Library.*

SARAH FULL HILL

W hile a funeral train was crossing the nation to bring the body of President Abraham Lincoln home to Illinois, the steamer *Sultana* was carrying ill and wounded Union soldiers north from Vicksburg. On April 27, 1865, the boat exploded, burned, and sank killing more than 1,500, including Union soldiers who had been imprisoned at the notorious Andersonville Prison. As a volunteer nurse, Sarah Hill witnessed the arrival of the survivors at the St. Louis riverfront.

The Southern prisons were being emptied and our poor men who had been confined in them were sent as fast as possible to their homes. Many of them were taken to Vicksburg from Andersonville and sent North on steamboats to St. Louis. It was about this time that the Sultana, a large steamboat with over three thousand returning prisoners on board, was blown up at Memphis. . . . The survivors were placed on other boats and sent up the river to St. Louis. . . . [Sarah and fellow volunteer nurses] went to the boat landing with soup and coffee and refreshments, for we knew in their journey up the river they had suffered untold hardships, many being rescued from drowning and many badly injured. When the boats tied up and the men began coming off, and we saw what the South had sent back to us from their prison pens, a groan of horror broke from us . . . those poor creatures, hardly the semblance of men, just spectres and wraiths. It broke our hearts and for a few moments we were overcome and wept in grief and rage. Words cannot express the horrors of their condition, poor starved diseased creatures, and then when home and freedom were in sight, to be drowned, slaughtered and slain in so terrible a manner. It was all too horrible.

From her family cottage on the northwest fringes of the city (now the Fairground Park neighborhood of St. Louis City) near Benton Barracks, Sarah chronicled the slow return of the veterans.

Daily now regiments were arriving and going out to Benton Barracks. They marched out on the street within a half block of our house and we were greatly impressed in noting the difference in the return of our men. Grim and quiet they marched, no bands playing, an occasional shrill fife and drum, and those were but few. All the gay military trappings conspicuous by their absence, but the work they started out to do was successfully completed. Our country was saved and was one, undivided, and they had given the best years of their manhood to accomplish it.

On July 22, Sarah's own Eben Marvin Hill came riding down that road, along with his "Engineer boys." Sarah was with her son, Georgie, and their young daughter, a "fine healthy child" born in February of 1865.

At last, E.M. wrote that they were starting for home, and we watched and waited. One hot morning on July 22nd, we were sitting on the shady stoop with my two babies. Soon we heard shouts and cheers and a band of soldiers was marching by on the street at the end of our block. Something about them looked familiar, and I remarked to Mother they looked like the Engineer boys. Just then an officer on horseback left the ranks and came galloping down the street. Georgie shrilled, "Why that's Snorter. That's my Papa's horse. Why that's my Papa," and out he rushed to meet him. We hardly knew E.M. He was in full dress uniform. The trappings of his horse were so gay, so unlike what George and I were accustomed to when he was on active duty. But the boys were all going in full dress marching uniforms to be mustered out. E.M. could not refrain from coming to us for a minute as he rode by, and greeted us all joyfully, then rejoined his men.

That evening my soldier came home to me, unbuckled his

sword, laid off his uniform, his work for his country completed after four years of faithful service. He was just plain citizen Hill once more. The war was over and we were ready to begin life anew.

Hill, 330–34.